DEPARTMENT OF THE INTERIOR

UNITED STATES GEOLOGICAL SURVEY

GEORGE OTIS SMITH, Director

BULLETIN 494

THE

NEW MADRID EARTHQUAKE

BY

MYRON L. FULLER

WASHINGTON

GOVERNMENT PRINTING OFFICE

1912

ISBN 0-934426-49-X   The New Madrid Earthquake by Myron Fuller
Foreword and Cover Story by David Stewart
Cover Design by Daniel Reiff. Cover Art by Mark Farmer.

Fourth Edition. 1995. Reprinted by Gutenberg-Richter Publications from original 1912 version without revision or modification.
Price: $15.95

Copies available from: Gutenberg-Richter Publications
Rt. 1, Box 646
Marble Hill, MO 63764
(573) 238-4273 or (800) 758-8629

Other Books Available from Gutenberg-Richter Publications:

The Earthquake America Forgot, Stewart/Knox, 376 pp. Hard cover.	$29.95
The Earthquake that Never Went Away, Stewart/Knox, 222 pp., Soft.	19.95
The New Madrid Fault Finders Guide, Knox/Stewart, 181 pp., Soft cover.	16.95
Effects of Earthquakes in Central U.S., Nuttli, 50 pp, Soft cover.	9.95
150 Earthquake Slides on the New Madrid Fault, Stewart/Knox	180.00
Damages & Losses from Future NM Earthquakes. Stewart, 74 pp., Soft.	*FREE
Earthquake Guide to Home & Office. Dillard/Stewart, 12 pp. Booklet	**FREE

Please Add $3.00 shipping and Handling for first book, $1.50 for second, $1.00 per book thereafter. * Although "Damages & Losses" is Free, normal shipping charges apply. **For the Earthquake Guide add $1.00 postage unless request included with order.   CHECK, MASTER CARD or VISA OK
WRITE OR CALL FOR FREE PUBLICATION CATALOGUE

Publishers Cataloging in Publication
(*Prepared by Quality Books, Inc.*)

Fuller, Myron L.
The New Madrid earthquake / by Myron L. Fuller; foreword and cover story by David Stewart. -- 4th ed.
p. cm
"A scientific factual field account"--Cover.
Originally published: Washington: Government Printing Office, 1912, in: U.S. Geological Survey bulletin ; 494.
"Reprinted from original 1912 version without revision or modification by Gutenberg-Richter Publications, Marble Hill, Missouri, 1995" -- Verso.
Includes bibliographical references and index.
ISBN 0-934426-9-X
1. Earthquakes--Missouri--New Madrid Region.
I. Stewart, David, 1937 Sept 20-   II. Title.   III. Title: U.S. Geological Survey bulletin ; 494.

QE535.2.U6F85 1995   551.2'2'09778985
                                                QB195-20380

FOREWORD

Scientists today understand a great deal more about the nature of the New Madrid Seismic Zone than was known even a few decades ago. Much has come by way of the dense network of seismographic stations installed in the early 1970's and administrated by St. Louis University, Memphis State University and the U.S. Geological Survey (USGS).

This book was originally published by the USGS as Bulletin 494 in 1912. Although printed a century after the fact, this work is singularly important. It was the first systematic attempt to compile a comprehensive scientific account and field survey of the effects for the hundreds of tremors that visited the Mississippi Valley in 1811-12. This document is the starting point used by all researchers and historians on the subject.

Myron Fuller accomplished an admirable feat in the thoroughness with which he assembled facts available in 1912. Some things held tentative in his day have now been confirmed. For example, Fuller was uncertain about the credibility of reports that the Earth gave off flashing, glowing lights during the shaking. He also was unsure about the reports of the Mississippi River flowing backwards and forming temporary waterfalls. Today, historians have established the authenticity of the retrograde river flow, as well as the waterfalls. That earthquakes can produce light has been confirmed in many places throughout the world, and scientists have not only photographed them but have a physical explanation. Seismoluminescence occurs when quartz crystals are repeatedly squeezed. Quartz sands underlay the entire New Madrid Seismic Zone and could be expected to emit earthquake lights when compressed by seismic waves.

Fuller also was unable to produce a reliable count of the events from data available to him, and discrepancies exist in the various news reports and journal records he compiled. However, starting with Fuller's work and relocating his sources plus many others, the late Dr. Otto Nuttli has produced a count of the events and assigned the following Richter surface wave magnitudes (M_S): More than 2,000 events occurred between December 16, 1811 and the end of March 1812. On December 16, 1811 three great events occurred one of $M_S = 8.6$ at 2:30 a.m., one of $M_S = 8.0$ at 8:15 a.m., and another of $M_S = 8.0$ at noon. On January 23, 1812, an earthquake of $M_S = 8.4$ occurred and in February another great quake of $M_S = 8.8$ occurred. Thus, by Dr. Nuttli's count, during a five month period there occurred five great quakes of $M_S = 8.0$ or larger, 15 of $M_S = 6.7$-7.7, 35 of about $M_S = 5.9$, 65 of about 5.3, 89 of about $m_b = 5.0$ and some 1,800 in the range of $m_b = 3.0$-4.5 magnitudes.

Fuller's book was out of print for many years. It came back into being briefly during the 1950's when published by a private individual in Cape Girardeau, Missouri, under the signet of Ramfree Press. The Central United States Earthquake Consortium in cooperation with the National Center Earthquake Engineering Research in Buffalo, New York, printed a limited edition in December 1988, also now out of print. For years the most available copies were only to be found in libraries, often worn and yellowed with age. The Center for Earthquake Studies at Cape Girardeau, Missouri, reprinted the book in 1989 and 1990 but has not published it since. Gutenberg-Richter Publications plans to keep this important book in print for as long as there is a demand.

Dr. David Stewart
Former Director, Central U.S. Earthquake Consortium, Marion, Illinois
Founder and Former Director, Center for Earthquake Studies,
Southeast Missouri State University, Cape Girardeau, Missouri
August 1995

CONTENTS.

3

CONTENTS.

ILLUSTRATIONS.

THE NEW MADRID EARTHQUAKE.

By MYRON L. FULLER.

INTRODUCTION.

GENERAL STATEMENT.

The succession of shocks designated collectively the New Madrid earthquake occurred in an area of the central Mississippi Valley including southeastern Missouri, northeastern Arkansas, and western Kentucky and Tennessee. (See Pl. I and fig. 1.) Beginning December 16, 1811, and lasting more than a year, these shocks have not been surpassed or even equaled for number, continuance of disturbance, area affected, and severity by the more recent and better-known shocks at Charleston and San Francisco. As the region was almost unsettled at that time relatively little attention was paid to the phenomenon, the published accounts being few in number and incomplete in details. For these reasons, although scientific literature in this country and in Europe has given it a place among the great earthquakes of the world, the memory of it has lapsed from the public mind.

Shaler,[1] writing of the earthquake in 1869, said:

The occurrence of such a shock in a region like the Mississippi Valley, on the borders of a great river, is probably unprecedented in the history of earthquakes. * * * Many of the events of that convulsion were without a parallel.

Scientifically this earthquake may be regarded as a type, exhibiting in unusual detail the geologic effects of great disturbances upon unconsolidated deposits. For this reason its phenomena have an importance which, in the absence of any previous systematic discussion, warrants detailed consideration.

FIELD WORK AND ACKNOWLEDGMENTS.

The writer's attention was first called to the region by Prof. E. M. Shepard, who had become interested in it because of the relation between artesian conditions and certain effects of the earthquake, which had become apparent during an investigation of underground waters. In the fall of 1904 Prof. Shepard and the writer traversed

---

[1] Shaler, N. S., Earthquakes of the western United States: Atlantic Monthly, Nov., 1869, pp. 549-559.

in a dugout the sunk lands along Varney River, near Kennett, Mo.,
and later made a trip on horseback up the old De Soto trail and along
St. Francis River. The second trip was made under the guidance

FIGURE 1.—Map showing the extent of earthquake disturbances in the New Madrid area in 1811-12.
For additional records of the direction of vibrations see table, page 41.

of Mr. C. B. Baily, city engineer of Wynne, Ark., who from timber
explorations had become familiar with the earthquake features in the
still almost untouched forests north of the St. Louis, Iron Mountain &

Southern Railway between Memphis and Wynne. In the following year the writer, in connection with studies of underground water, covered most of the region reached by railroads in Arkansas and Missouri and made a wagon trip, again in company with Prof. Shepard, around Reelfoot Lake, in Tennessee. A short account embodying Prof. Shepard's observations appeared in 1905,[1] and a number of preliminary notes and popular papers by the writer have been published in magazines.[2]

In the present report an attempt is made to present a systematic record of some of the phenomena of this great earthquake, including both the contemporaneous and the present aspect of the resulting features.

THE STORY OF THE EARTHQUAKE.

SOURCES OF INFORMATION.

The story of the earthquake is told in two ways—in the quaint, picturesque, and graphic accounts of contemporaries, and in the equally striking geographic and geologic records, which even now may be clearly read at many points in the region. For the sake of brevity only a single general account compiled from the early descriptions will be presented, but in the bibliography (pp. 111-115) references to original publications containing detailed narratives are given. In the discussion of the physiographic phenomena many references to reports of the old writers will also be found.

The contemporary accounts are doubtless exaggerated, for calm observation and accurate recording of an earthquake is impossible if the shocks are severe and dangerous. It is interesting to note, however, that, except a few features, such as the flashes of light (doubtless resulting from the general belief in the volcanic origin of the disturbance), most of the reported phenomena have been verified by the recent investigations. Fortunately a number of scientists or men of education were in or near the region during the period of disturbance and have given vivid pictures of their experiences. John Bradbury, a noted English botanist, was on a flatboat on the Mississippi only a few miles below New Madrid at the time of the shock; Audubon, our own naturalist, was traveling in Kentucky; Capt. Roosevelt was taking down the river the first steamer to navigate western waters; L. Bringier, a well-known engineer and surveyor, was in the midst of the disturbance; Maj. Long's expedition was passing through the region on its way from Pittsburgh to the Rocky Mountains. Daniel Drake, at Cincinnati, and Jared Brooks, at

---

[1] The New Madrid earthquake: Jour. Geology, vol. 13, pp. 45-62.

[2] Causes and periods of earthquakes in the New Madrid area, Missouri and Arkansas: Science, new ser., vol. 21, 1905, pp. 349-350; Comparative intensities of the New Madrid, Charleston, and San Francisco earthquakes: Idem, vol. 23, 1905, pp. 917-918; Our greatest earthquakes: Pop. Sci. Monthly, July, 1906, pp. 76-86; Earthquakes and the forest: Forestry and Irrigation, vol. 12, 1906, pp. 261-267.

Louisville, kept careful records of the shocks, and S. L. Mitchill, geologist and Congressman, collected records from all parts of the country. While the resulting phenomena were still fresh the region was visited by our own geographer, Timothy Flint, and by Sir Charles Lyell, the great English geologist.

Lyell's visit was particularly fortunate, for he has given us a graphic description of the conditions 35 years after the disturbance, when the vegetation had not yet hidden the evidences of the movement. This description, with later observations on the geologic features, many of which are very pronounced, furnishes data of the greatest value and substantiates in almost every particular the early accounts.

SUMMARY OF THE DISASTER.

The evening of December 15, 1811, in the New Madrid area was clear and quiet, with no unusual conditions which could be regarded as portending the catastrophe soon to take place. A little after 2 o'clock on the morning of December 16, the inhabitants of the region were suddenly awakened by the groaning, creaking, and cracking of the timbers of the houses or cabins in which they were sleeping, by the rattle of furniture thrown down, and by the crash of falling chimneys. In fear and trembling they hurriedly groped their way from their houses to escape the falling débris, and remained shivering in the winter air until morning, the repeated shocks at intervals during the night keeping them from returning to their weakened or tottering dwellings. Daylight brought little improvement to their situation, for early in the morning another shock, preceded by a low rumbling and fully as severe as the first, was experienced. The ground rose and fell as earth waves, like the long, low swell of the sea, passed across its surface, tilting the trees until their branches interlocked and opening the soil in deep cracks as the surface was bent. Landslides swept down the steeper bluffs and hillsides; considerable areas were uplifted, and still larger areas sunk and became covered with water emerging from below through fissures or little "craterlets" or accumulating from the obstruction of the surface drainage. On the Mississippi great waves were created, which overwhelmed many boats and washed others high upon the shore, the return current breaking off thousands of trees and carrying them out into the river. High banks caved and were precipitated into the river, sand bars and points of islands gave way, and whole islands disappeared.

During December 16 and 17 shocks continued at short intervals but gradually diminished in intensity. They occurred at longer intervals until January 23, when there was another shock, similar in intensity and destructiveness to the first. This shock was followed by about two weeks of quiescence, but on February 7 there were several alarming and destructive shocks, the last equaling or surpassing any previous disturbance, and for several days the earth was in a nearly constant tremor.

For fully a year from this date small shocks occurred at intervals of a few days, but as there were no other destructive shocks the people gradually became accustomed to the vibrations and gave little or no further attention to them.

PREVIOUS EARTHQUAKES IN THE MISSISSIPPI VALLEY.

That the shock known as the New Madrid earthquake was not the first felt in the region is shown by written records, by Indian traditions, and by geologic evidence.

Recorded shocks.—Of the shocks felt by the early settlers the best summary is supplied by Drake. Speaking of the series of 1811–12 he says:[1]

The shocks of this protracted series are not all which this country has sustained since it has been the abode of civilized man. We have certain accounts of five others.

The first was in the year 1776. Mr. John Heckewelder, then a missionary of the United Brethren, on the Muskingum River, in this State, has politely favored me with a memorandum concerning it. He does not recollect the month, but it was in the summer, and about 8 o'clock a. m. Its duration was two or three minutes. The southwest side of the house was raised with such violence that the furniture of the room was nearly overturned. It was accompanied with a subterranean rumbling noise. Early in the morning the weather was fair, but previous to the shock it began to thicken in the southwest. The cattle were frightened by the shake, and the Indians continued, after it, to apprehend some great disaster, of which they conceived this to be the precursor.

The second shock was in the year 1791 or 1792. I am unable to ascertain the precise time, but think it occurred in the month of April or May, about 7 o'clock in the morning. The weather was fair and mild. The jar was sufficient to agitate the furniture of the house. A rumbling noise in the earth, which seemed to pass from west to east, preceded the shake. It was, I believe, generally felt through the northern and northeastern parts of Kentucky, but whether beyond them I have not been able to learn.

The third shock occurred, as I am informed by George Turner, Esq., about 3 o'clock a. m. January 8, 1795, at Kaskaskia, Illinois Territory. It was also, I believe, felt in some parts of Kentucky. Its duration he estimates at a minute and a half. Its direction was nearly west and east. A subterranean noise attended, resembling that of many carriages driven rapidly over a pavement.

A fourth shock was experienced, we are informed by Prof. Barton,[2] at the Falls of Niagara, about 6 o'clock on the morning of the 26th of December, 1796. It appeared to come from the northwest and did not last more than two seconds, but was sensibly felt for 50 miles around the Falls.

The fifth and only additional shock of which I have been furnished with any certain accounts, occurred in the southern neighborhood of Lake Michigan, at 10 minutes past 2 o'clock p. m. on the 20th of August, 1804. At Fort Dearborn, on the bank of the lake, it was severe. From the report of Capt. William Whistler, it must have been a stronger throe than any experienced at this place. It was succeeded by a

---

[1] Drake, Daniel, Natural and statistical view or picture of Cincinnati, Cincinnati, 1815, pp. 243–244.
[2] Philadelphia Medical and Physical Journal, vol. 1.

short hurricane from the lake. At Fort Wayne, lying considerably to the east-south-east, it was less violent. John Johnston, Esq., my informant, remarks that the day at that place was clear and warm, without any unusual appearance. The general course of the earthquake was undoubtedly that of a line passing through those two forts.

Indian traditions.—Lyell records [1] that the Indians of the Mississippi Valley had a tradition of a great earthquake which had previously devastated the same region, but he concluded from the absence of old sink holes and of dead trees that no convulsion of similar magnitude could have occurred for many centuries previous to 1811. As shown in the following paragraphs he was mistaken in regard to the absence of such indications of previous shocks, for although it appears to be true that no fallen timber remained, there are many conspicuous and unquestionable geologic evidences of earlier disturbances.

Geologic evidence.—The geologic evidence of shocks long antedating that of 1811 is very conclusive, as has elsewhere been pointed out by the writer. [2] Cracks as large as any of those of the last great disturbance have been seen with trees fully 200 years old grown on their bottoms and slopes (Pl. II, *A*) indicating early shocks of an intensity equal to if not greater than that of the last. Nor is the action apparently altogether recent, for post-Lafayette but pre-Iowan faults (antedating the deposition of the loess), and apparently being either a cause or accompaniment of earthquakes, have been observed by the writer in Crowley Ridge, and Glenn has described [3] sandstone dikes filling old earthquake cracks in the Porters Creek formation of the Eocene Tertiary.

Other geologic evidence leading to the same conclusion is seen in the Tiptonville, Blytheville, and Little River domes and in the occurrence of certain sand sloughs. The Tiptonville dome is known to have antedated, in part at least, the shocks of 1811, as several writers mention that previous to this earthquake the land at New Madrid was never overflowed. This would not have been the case if it had been a part of the undisturbed flood plain. The erosion of the Blytheville and Little River domes since their uplift has been considerable (p. 64) and took place almost entirely before the 1811 shocks. If these domes are classed as earthquake features, as apparently they should be, from the description of the additional uplift of the Tiptonville dome which took place in 1811, it follows that the original disturbance must have long antedated the New Madrid earthquake. South of Lake St. Francis, as described elsewhere (p. 84),

[1] Lyell, Charles, A second visit to the United States of North America, London, 1849, p. 238.

[2] Causes and periods of earthquakes in the New Madrid area, Missouri and Arkansas: Science, new ser. vol. 21, 1905, pp. 349–350. Our greatest earthquakes: Pop. Sci. Monthly, July, 1906, p. 86.

[3] Glenn, L. C., Underground waters of Tennessee and Kentucky west of Tennessee River: Water-Supply Paper U. S. Geol. Survey, No. 164, 1906, pp. 30–31.

A. VIEW OF ONE SIDE OF FAULT TRENCH OR "FISSURE" NEAR BANKS OF ST. FRANCIS
RIVER, ARK

B. LANDSLIDE TRENCH AND RIDGE RESULTING FROM THE NEW MADRID EARTHQUAKE,
CHICKASAW BLUFFS, TENN.

several sloughs exist, which have all the characteristics of sunk lands except the dead timber, and are apparently true earthquake features. The absence of dead timber, such as characterizes the areas which sunk in 1811, however, points to a considerably earlier origin.

RECORD OF THE SHOCKS.

ATMOSPHERIC CONDITIONS PRECEDING FIRST SHOCK.

There is apparently no possible relation between earthquake shocks and weather, but it is not impossible that the variations in barometric pressure accompanying cyclonic movements of the atmosphere may occasionally be a factor. No barometric records are available for the time of the first New Madrid shock, and the atmospheric pressure can only be inferred from the weather conditions. The best information available is that afforded by the accounts of S. L. Mitchill,[1] C. L. Latrobe,[2] Daniel Drake,[3] and John Hayward.[4] From their descriptions it appears that nothing occurred in any way suggestive to scientific minds of unusual conditions, although it is fairly well established that immediately before the earthquake unusual warmth and a thick oppressive atmosphere with occasional rain and unseasonable thunder showers prevailed over a wide area of country. Near the immediate point of origin of the shocks, however, the weather seems to have been clear.

The records of the shock as preserved in contemporary literature are meager, but the writer has been able to obtain, chiefly from the compilation of Jared Brooks,[5] a list of some 250 shocks which took place in the six months following the one on December 16, 1811. The chief items of interest are given below.

TIME OF THE SHOCKS.

The exact time of the earthquake shocks must apparently remain in doubt, for, so far as is known, not a single exact determination was made. No seismographs were in existence, and as all of the principal shocks occurred in the middle of the night, when the consultation of reliable chronometers was impracticable, nothing was available but personal clocks or watches. These were all supposed to be set by local time, but as the longitude of few of the places had been accurately determined, and in most localities no special attempt to fix the true sun time had been made, the times given in the table must be considered as only approximately correct.

---

[1] A detailed narrative of the earthquakes which occurred on the 16th day of December, 1811: Trans. Lit. and Philos. Soc. New York, vol. 1, 1815, pp. 281–307.

[2] The rambler in North America, 2d ed., vol. 1, London, 1836, p. 107.

[3] Natural and statistical view or picture of Cincinnati, Cincinnati, 1815, pp. 239–242.

[4] Natural and aboriginal history of Tennessee, etc., Nashville, 1823, p. 124.

[5] McMurtrie, H., Sketches of Louisville and its environs, Louisville, 1819, Appendix.

The reported times of the three principal shocks are given in the following table. Something of the general rate of transmission may be determined from them, but the data are too inaccurate to warrant an attempt to construct coseismal lines.

Reported times of principal shocks.

Locality.	Shock of Dec. 16.[a]	Shock of Jan. 23.[b]	Shock of Feb. 7.[c]
	a. m.	*a. m.*	*a. m.*
Annapolis, Md			
Augusta, Ky		9. 44	
Baltimore, Md			3. 20
Cape Girardeau, Mo			4. 00
Charleston, S. C	2. 00		
Chillicothe, Ohio		9. 15	
Cincinnati, Ohio	2. 15		3. 30
Columbia, S. C	2. 20		
Edenton, N. C	3. 00		
Frankfort, Ky		9. 15	
Lexington, Ky	2. 35	8. 50	3. 40
Little Prairie, Mo		8. 40	3. 30
Louisville, Ky	2. 00		
Meadville, Pa	2. 15	8. 50	3. 15
New Madrid, Mo	3. 00		
Pittsburgh, Pa	2. 00		
Richmond, Va			4. 00
Ste. Genevieve, Mo		9. 30	3. 55
Savannah, Ga			3. 00
Washington, D. C	2. 50		
			4. 00

a Referred to meridian of Richmond.
b Referred to meridian of New York.   c Referred to meridian of Philadelphia.

CENTER OF DISTURBANCE.

Two lines of evidence are available for determining the position of the center of disturbance: (1) The completeness of the destruction of buildings and the extent of geologic and physiographic changes, and (2) the recorded direction of movements.

Earlier shock.—In the first shock by far the greatest destruction occurred in the heavily-shaded area on figure 1, with minor damage in the lightly-shaded areas along the rivers. The directions of vibration in the outlying towns, which are fairly accordant, also point to an origin in the heavily-shaded area or in the vicinity of New Madrid. In view of the fact that the waves at New Madrid and along the Mississippi were from the west, it seems certain that the centrum was west of the river.

Shaler, on the basis of statements attributed to the Indians that "in the region between the Mississippi and the great plains forests were overthrown, rocks split asunder," etc., placed the "seismic vertex of the New Madrid shocks much to the west of the Mississippi."[1]

As a matter of fact it is probable that the "great plains" referred to are the extensive prairies just west of Crowley Ridge. At any rate, it is now apparent that the effects of the shocks were much less in the region west of the ridge than in the area between the ridge and the Mississippi.

[1] Shaler, N. S., Earthquakes of the western United States: Atlantic Monthly, Nov., 1869, pp. 551, 552.

The shock is believed to have proceeded from a northeast-southwest fault, as shown in Plate I, located approximately 15 miles west of the river. This is a few miles farther west than the point given by the contemporary writers, namely, either New Madrid or Little Prairie (now Caruthersville) a few miles below, at which point the destruction was most complete. At that time the effects of the shock in the unsettled regions back from the river, in which the new position has been determined, were little known.

Subsequent shocks.—The few recorded directions of the shock of December 17 seem on the whole to favor a centrum in the same area. The shock of January 23 was instrumentally recorded as from the south-southeast at Cincinnati. It was, however, one of the most violent of the series at New Madrid, doing much damage, but the country to the east, where, on the basis of Cincinnati determinations, the centrum should have been, was little affected. It is therefore probable that the shock originated, as the earlier ones had, in the New Madrid area, the abnormal direction at Cincinnati being explained, perhaps, by local causes.

Of the three "great shocks" of February 7 at Cincinnati, the first two were from the southwest or south-southwest—that is, from the direction of New Madrid—the subsequent shock being from the south-southeast. Like the shock on January 23, this one may have been affected in direction by local causes, perhaps by a reflected motion from the Appalachian mountain mass. It is not impossible, however, that new centers of disturbance were formed during this and other of the later shocks, for though the disturbances at New Madrid were little greater than the earlier shocks they were decidedly stronger in the outlying eastward districts, the distances to which the vibrations extended being considerably greater. From these or similar evidences Shaler concluded that, although during the first part of the series of shocks the center of the disturbance was west of New Madrid, "the point of greatest frequency gradually moved eastward until it was near the mouth of the Wabash River in the Ohio Valley. Here, over a region about 20 miles in diameter, a succession of shocks occurred for more than two years, during which time only a few days passed without bringing a distinct movement. Most of the oscillations were of such a slight character as not to be felt outside of this narrow district." [1]

There is, however, no evidence of great disturbances in the shape of faults, sand-blows, sunk lands, or domes, except in the New Madrid area. On the whole it seems probable, therefore, that all the severe shocks originated in the original area of disturbance, but it is not impossible that some of the smaller shocks may have had other foci, the vibrations originating in local readjustments due to the dis-

---

[1] Shaler, N. S., Earthquakes of the western United States: Atlantic Monthly, Nov., 1869, p. 556.

turbance of the equilibrium by the New Madrid shocks, either through the settling of the loose sediments of the valleys or minor slipping along fault planes in the harder rocks. The vertical shocks at Detroit and Cincinnati on May 8 may thus represent local readjustments following the severe general disturbance of the day before. At the United States Saline, Ill., shocks were felt almost daily for two years, but in general they were seldom felt at Shawneetown, only 12 miles away. Some of the more severe shocks, however, were felt at this town as well as at Kaskaskia and along Wabash River.[1] It should be emphasized, however, that although the shocks mentioned may be of local origin it is not improbable that they were the result of the disturbance of local geologic conditions by the New Madrid vibrations.

AREA AFFECTED.

The area affected by the New Madrid earthquake may be subdivided into an area of marked earth disturbances, an area of slight earth disturbances, and an area of tremors only. In the first is included the territory characterized by pronounced earthquake phenomena, such as domes and sunk lands, fissures, sinks, sand blows, large landslides, etc. This district includes the New Madrid region, originally considered a relatively small area, including the villages of New Madrid and Little Prairie (Caruthersville). It is now known, however, to be somewhat larger, extending from a point west of Cairo on the north to the latitude of Memphis on the south, a distance of more than 100 miles, and from Crowley Ridge on the west to Chickasaw Bluffs on the east, a distance of over 50 miles. The total area characterized by disturbances of the type mentioned is from 30,000 to 50,000 square miles.

In the area of slight earth disturbances will be included districts in which such minor features as the caving of banks, etc., took place. We have records in the narratives of Latrobe [2] and others of the occurrence of such phenomena along the Mississippi and Ohio, while Bradbury [3] records similar disturbances as far down the Mississippi as the mouth of the St. Francis, near Helena. The disappearance of island 94 near Vicksburg has been described by August Warner.[4] In fact, there is little doubt that such phenomena as caving were prominent northward nearly to Herculaneum, northeastward to a point beyond the Wabash, and southward at least to the mouth of the Arkansas. Although no records from the White River region have been seen, it was probably included in the area of slight disturbance, and it is so shown in figure 1. It is also possible that the lower Arkansas was affected to some extent.

[1] Drake, Daniel, Natural and statistical view or picture of Cincinnati, Cincinnati, 1815, p. 238.
[2] Latrobe, C. J. The rambler in North America, 2d edition, vol. 1, London, 1836.
[3] Bradbury, John, Early western travels, Cleveland, 1904, vol. 5, pp. 204-210.
[4] Warner, August, quoted in Am. Geologist, vol. 30, p. 83.

The area of tremors was naturally far more extensive. On the north they are reported to have been felt in "Upper Canada," on the northwest they are reported to have been felt by the Indians in the region of the upper portions of the Missouri country,[1] and in the region between the headwaters of the Arkansas and the Missouri, a distance of more than 500 miles from New Madrid. Southwestward the shocks were felt in the Red River settlements and on the Washita River, an equal distance from the center of disturbance. To the south the shock was felt at New Orleans, also 500 miles distant; to the northeast at Detroit, 600 miles away; and to the east at Washington, over 700 miles, and at Boston, 1,100 miles distant. A total area of over 1,000,000 square miles, or half that of the entire United States, was so disturbed that the vibrations could be felt without the aid of instruments.

GENERAL DESTRUCTIVENESS OF THE SHOCKS.

The severity of the shocks was such as to ruin the country in the central area of disturbance for years. After the earthquake had moderated, according to Flint,[2] the country—

exhibited a melancholy aspect of chasms, of sand covering the earth, of trees thrown down, or lying at an angle of 45°, or split in the middle. The earthquakes still recurred at short intervals, so that the people had no confidence to rebuild good houses, or chimneys of brick.

The people of Little Prairie (Caruthersville), who suffered most—

had their settlement—which consisted of a hundred families and which was located in a wide and very deep and fertile bottom—broken up. When I passed it, and stopped to contemplate the traces of the catastrophe which remained after seven years, the crevices where the earth had burst were sufficiently manifest, and the whole region was covered with sand to the depth of 2 or 3 feet. The surface was red with oxided pyrites of iron, and the sand blows, as they were called, were abundantly mixed with this kind of earth, and with pieces of pit coal. But two families remained of the whole settlement. * * * When I resided there, this district, formerly so level, rich, and beautiful, had the most melancholy of all aspect of decay, the tokens of former cultivation and habitancy, which were now mementos of desolation and desertion. Large and beautiful orchards, left uninclosed, houses uninhabited, deep chasms in the earth, obvious at frequent intervals—such was the face of the country, although the people had for years become so accustomed to frequent and small shocks, which did no essential injury, that the lands were gradually rising again in value, and New Madrid was slowly rebuilding, with frail buildings, adapted to the apprehensions of the people.

NUMBER AND DISTRIBUTION OF THE SHOCKS.

The number and distribution of the principal shocks can be best presented by means of a table such as is given below. It should be borne in mind that numerous as the recorded shocks are, they are

---

[1] James, Edwin, Account of an expedition from Pittsburgh to the Rocky Mountains, Philadelphia, 1823, vol. 1, p. 272.

[2] Flint, Timothy, Recollections of the last ten years, Boston, 1826, pp. 225, 227.

but a small part of the number that would have been recorded if there had been any seismographs in the zone of disturbance. Unfortunately, however, no instruments existed in the region except some homemade apparatus at Cincinnati, and only those shocks strong enough to be felt or to affect objects visibly are in general noted.

Record of the shocks of the New Madrid earthquake.[1]

Authority.	Locality.	Date.	Hour.	Remarks.
Bradbury..	Between New Madrid and mouth of St. Francis River.	Dec. 16, 1811	2 a. m.............	Violent; boat nearly upset; trees fell; banks caved.
	....do..............	....do........	2.30 or after.......	Terrible, but not equal to first.
	....do..............	....do........	Intervals of 6 to 10 minutes during night; 27 shocks before daylight.	Slight compared with first and second.
	....do..............	....do........	Daylight..........	Equal to first; same phenomena.
	....do..............	....do........	Breakfast.........	Very severe; nearly thrown down.
	....do..............	....do........	After breakfast....	Man nearly thrown into river.
	....do..............	....do........	11 a. m............	Violent; trees shaken; banks fell; river agitated.
	....do..............	Dec. 17, 1811	5 a. m.............	
	....do..............	....do........	7 a. m.............	
	....do..............	....do........	12 noon	Severe and of long duration.
	....do..............	....do........	7.30 p. m.........	
	....do..............	Dec. 18, 1811	3 to 4 a. m........	
	....do..............	....do........	6 a. m............	
	....do..............	....do........	12 noon	Violent and of long duration; trees thrown into river.
	....do..............	....do........	6 p. m............	Slight.
	....do..............	....do........	9 p. m............	Do.
	....do..............	Dec. 19, 1811	11................	
	....do..............	{Dec. 19, (18?), 1811.	}5 p. m.	
	....do..............	Dec. 20, 1811	7 p. m............	
	....do..............	Dec. 21, 1811	4.30 a. m..........	Not very violent, but lasted nearly a minute.
Bryan......	New Madrid......	Jan. 23, 1812	....	As violent as worst of preceding.
	....do..............	{Jan. 23, 1812 to Feb. 4, 1812	}	Shocks frequent.
	....do..............	Feb. 4, 1812	....	Nearly as severe as any.
	....do..............	Feb. 5, 1812	....	4 shocks, severe.
Lesieur....	....do..............	Feb. 7, 1812	....	Known as hard shock.
	....do..............	Dec. 16, 1811	2 a. m.............	
	....do..............	....do........	7 a. m.............	
	....do..............	June 7, 1812	....	As severe as first.
	....do..............	Feb. 7, 1812	....	Big shock.
Mitchill....	Cape Girardeau...	Nov. 9, 1812	4 p. m.............	Considerable motion to furniture.
	Washington.......	Dec. 16, 1811	3 a. m.............	Strong enough to shake windows and furniture.
	....do..............	....do........	6 a. m.............	Do.
	....do..............	....do........	8 a. m.............	Light.
	Richmond.........	....do........	3 a. m.............	Shook houses and furniture and rang bells.
	....do..............	....do........	6 a. m.............	Do.
	....do..............	....do........	8 a. m.............	Do.
	Norfolk and Portsmouth, Va.	....do........	3 a. m.............	Stopped clocks, rattled doors, swung hanging objects.
	....do..............	....do........	8 a. m.............	Do.
	Raleigh, N. C....	....do........	2 to 3 a. m	Several shocks distinctly felt.
	....do..............	....do........	3 to 7 a. m	Several faint shocks.
	Georgetown, S. C.	....do........	3 to 8 a. m	Severe; upset tub of water, etc.
	....do..............	Dec. 18, 1811	12 noon	Slight.
	Columbia, S. C....	Dec. 16, 1811	2.30 a. m..........	Houses rocked; plaster fell; dogs barked; heavy shock followed by 3 light ones.
	....do..............	....do........	8 a. m.............	2 shocks.
	....do..............	....do........	10 a. m............	Light.
	....do..............	Dec. 17, 1811	12.15 p. m.........	Smart shock.
	Laurens and Newberry, S. C.	....do........	12.15 p. m.........	Cracked chimneys.
	Charleston, S. C...	Dec. 16, 1811	3 a. m.............	Lasted 2 to 3 minutes; bells rang; clocks stopped; well water roiled; buildings shaken.
	....do..............	....do........	8 a. m.............	Do.

[1] Except at Louisville, for which see more detailed table, pp. 22-26.

Record of the shocks of the New Madrid earthquake—Continued.

Authority.	Locality.	Date.	Hour.	Remarks.
Mitchill	Charleston, S. C...	Dec. 16, 1811	8.15 a. m..........	Light.
	Savannah, Ga....	....do........	2 to 3 a. m	Lasted 1 minute; motion enough to make walking difficult; another soon after.
	....do..............	....do........	8 a. m.............	Slight.
	....do.............	Dec. 17, 1811	12 noon	Do.
	Natchez, Miss.....	Dec. 16, 1811	2.10 a. m..........	Clocks stopped; objects fell; walls cracked; river agitated; trees waved.
	Piney River, Tenn	....do......	....	Banks of river caved; chimney thrown down.
	....do..............	Dec. 17, 1811	....	4 shocks.
	....do.............	Dec. 18, 1811 to Dec. 30, 1811	....	1 or more daily.
	Knoxville, Tenn..	Dec. 16, 1811	2 a. m.............	Lasted 3 minutes; windows and furniture shaken.
	....do..............	Dec. 16, 1811	2.30 a. m..........	One-half minute.
	....do.............	Dec. 16, 1811	Early morning....	Three slight shocks.
	Columbia, Tenn...	....do........	2 to 3 a. m	Wakened people.
	Jeffersonville, Ind.	....do........	2 a. m.............	Moved furniture.
	Vincennes, Ind....	....do........	2 a. m.............	Severe shock.
	Red Bank, Ind....	....do........	2.30 a. m	Violent; chimney wrecked.
	....do.....	....do........	Sunrise...........	Do.
	St. Louis, Mo....	....do........	2.15 a. m	Shook buildings; chimneys thrown down.
	....do..............	....do........	2.47 a. m	Do.
	....do.............	....do........	3.34 a. m..........	As heavy as first.
	....do.............	....do........	Daylight..........	
	....do.............	....do........	8 a. m.............	
	....do.............	....do........	11.30 a. m.........	
	Lebanon, Ohio...	....do........	2 a. m.............	People left houses.
	Archville, Ohio...	....do........	2 and 8 a. m......	Woke people.
	Henderson County, Ky.	....do........	2 a. m.............	Overturned nearly all chimneys.
	Detroit, Mich.....	Dec. 17, 1811	....	
	Herculaneum, Mo.	Dec. 16, 1811	2 a. m.............	Lasted 10 to 12 minutes; severe; buildings wrecked.
	....do..............	....do........	3 a. m.............	
	....do.............	....do........	Daylight..........	Cradles rocked; bells rang; chimneys broken.
	Carthage, Tenn...	Dec. 16–Jan. 1	....	Shocks daily.
	....do.............	Jan. 1, 1812	3.30 a. m (?).......	Bricks thrown from chimney.
	Henderson, Ark...	Dec. 16, 1811	2 a. m.............	Shocks felt by Indians.
	New Orleans, La..	....do......	....	Weak.
	Philadelphia, Pa..	....do......	....	Doubtful.
	New York.......	....do......	....	Do.
	Newark, N. J.....	....do......	....	Several shocks felt.
	Washington, D. C.	Jan. 23, 1812	9 a. m.............	Similar to that of Dec. 16.
	Nottingham, Ind..	....do........	9.20 a. m..........	1 minute; buildings shook.
	Richmond, Va....	....do........	9.30 a. m..........	Books nearly thrown from shelves; people stopped eating.
	Coshocton, Ohio...			Felt.
	Georgetown, Louisville, and Frankfort, Ky.			Do.
	Chillicothe, Ohio..			Do.
	Charleston, S. C...	Jan. 23, 1812	9.15 a. m..........	Severest felt.
	New York........	....do......	....	Reported by papers.
	Detroit, Mich.....	Feb. 3, 1812	4.15 p. m..........	Small.
	....do.............	Feb. 7, 1812	4 p. m.............	Lasted 1½ minutes; nearly equaled that of Dec. 16.
	....do.............	....do........	7.30 p. m..........	Small.
	....do.............	....do........	9.55 p. m..........	Do.
	....do.............	....do........	11 p. m...........	Do.
	....do.............	Feb. 8, 1812	2 a. m.............	Vertical motion.
	Pittsburgh, Pa....	Feb. 7, 1812	4 a. m.............	Alarming; severest yet felt.
	Livingston County, Ky.	Feb. 8, 1812	a. m.............	Horse refused to proceed.
	Bardstown, Ky...			Fissures and ejections.
	Georgia...........	Dec. 23, 1811	a. m.............	Severe shaking.
	....do.............	Feb. 7, 1812	a. m.............	Do.
	....do.............	Feb. 16, 1812	a. m.............	Do.
	Clarksville, Tenn..	Dec. 14, 1812	a. m.............	Fairly severe.
James......	Red River........			Principal shocks felt.
	Washita River....			Do.
	Middlebury, Vt...			Shocks in winter.
Drake......	St. Genevieve, Mo.			500 shocks.
	U. S. Saline, Ill...			Daily local shocks.
	Cincinnati........	Dec. 16, 1811	2.24 a. m..........	Strong; lasted 6 to 7 minutes; moved furniture; broke tops from chimneys.

Record of the shocks of the New Madrid earthquake—Continued.

Authority.	Locality.	Date.	Hour.	Remarks.
Drake.....	Cincinnati	Dec. 16,1811	3 a. m............	Slight vibrations.
	....do............	....do......	7.20 a. m..........	Moderate rocking, terminating in strong throe.
	...do............	....do......	7.30 a. m..........	Slight oscillations.
	....do............	....do.......	10 to 11 a. m......	Do.
	....do............	Dec. 17,1811	11.43 a. m.........	Stronger than last.
	....do............	Dec. 18,1811	11.30 a. m.........	Moderate agitation.
	....do............	Dec. 31,1811	4 to 5 a. m........	A few gentle rockings.
	....do............	Jan. 3,1812	2 to 3 a. m.......	Slight vibrations.
	....do............	Jan. 23,1812	9 a. m............	Great number of strong undulations in quick succession, lasting 4 or 5 minutes.
	....do............	Jan. 27,1812	8.45 a. m..........	Solitary tremor as strong as that of Jan. 23.
	....do............	Feb. 4,1812	4 p. m............	A pretty strong agitation.
	....do............	Feb. 5–6,1812	All day...........	Many slight jars determined by plumb lines.
	....do............	Feb. 7,1812	3.45 p. m..........	Several alarming oscillations, the last surpassing all previous shocks; chimney tops thrown down; fissures formed.
	....do............	Feb. 8,1812	All day...........	Numerous very slight tremors.
	....do............	....do......	8 p. m............	Slight agitation.
	....do............	....do......	8.30 p. m..........	Vibration continuing nearly a minute.
	....do............	....do......	10.40 p. m........	Stronger than last; much trembling, but little oscillation.
	....do............	...do......	Night............	Numerous slight tremors.
	....do............	Feb. 10,1812	4 p. m............	Gentle vibration.
	....do............	Feb. 11,1812	1 a. m............	Do.
	....do............	....do......	6 a. m............	Do.
	....do............	Feb. 13,1812	10 a. m...........	Do.
	....do............	....do......	2 p. m............	Do.
	....do............	Feb. 16,1812	10 a. m (?)	Do.
	....do............	Feb. 17,1812	3.40 a. m.........	Strong shocks; undulation SSE. and NNW.
	....do............	Feb. 20,1812	10 to 11 p. m.....	Slight shocks.
	....do............	Feb. 21,1812	12.30 a. m........	A short but strong shock.
	....do............	Feb. 22,1812	3 to 4 a. m.......	Slight south to north vibration.
	....do............	Mar. 3,1812	6.30 a. m.........	A few slight rockings.
	....do............	Mar. 5,1812	6.10 a. m.........	Several short but strong rockings.
	..do............	Mar. 10,1812	8 p. m............	Strong vibration.
	....do............	Mar. 11,1812	2 to 3 a. m.......	Slight vibration.
	....do............	Apr. 30,1812	(?)...............	Moderate agitation.
	....do............	May 4,1812	11 a. m...........	Slight shock.
	....do............	May 10,1812	11 p. m...........	Do.
	....do............	June 25,1812	Night............	Slight agitation.
	....do............	June 26,1812	8 a. m............	2 slight vibrations.
	....do............	Sept. 15.1812	Daylight..........	Do.
	....do............	Dec. 22,1812	3 p. m............	Slight vibration.
	....do............	Mar. 6,1813	10 p. m...........	Very slight shock.
	....do............	Dec. 12,1813	10 to 11 a. m.....	Do.
	....do............	....do......	3 to 4 p. m.......	Do.

The fact that shocks are shown for distant localities where none are indicated at New Madrid probably arises from the fact that no systematic or continuous observations were made at the latter point and only a few fragmentary statements are available. It is, of course, a possibility that some of the more distant shocks were of local origin and unrelated to those of the New Madrid region. Other discrepancies arise from the fact that there were no self-recording instruments, and the lists indicate only those vibrations which could be felt or which happened to occur when the observers of the crude home-made pendulums were at hand.

EFFECTS OF THE SHOCKS OUTSIDE OF THE NEW MADRID AREA.

The following summary of the manifestations of the New Madrid earthquake, except those at Louisville and Cincinnati, is compiled mainly from the excellent narrative of Mitchill.[1]

MISSISSIPPI VALLEY.

The earthquake was felt at New Orleans, but was not severe. At Natchez four shocks were felt on the morning of December 16, the principal one being recorded as occurring at 2.10. Many houses were shaken, suspended objects swung to and fro, some plastered walls were cracked, a few articles fell from shelves, and several clocks were stopped. The surface of the river was agitated and parts of the banks fell in. The tops of the trees waved from side to side, but there seems to have been little or no noise.

Near Piney River, Tenn., 20 acres of land adjacent to the river subsided until the tops of the trees were level with the surrounding earth. At Knoxville the first shock of the 16th is reported to have lasted more than 3 minutes, rattling the windows and furniture and awakening the inhabitants. Half an hour later another shock, lasting half a minute, was experienced, while between sunrise and breakfast three others, each of a few seconds' duration, were felt. At Columbia, in the same State, the people were awakened by the principal shock, which lasted 10 to 15 minutes. It was accompanied by a peculiar sound, which appeared to proceed from the southwest to the northeast. At Carthage and vicinity, also in Tennessee, there were one or more shocks daily from December 16, 1811, to January 1, 1812. At 3.30 on the latter date a shock threw bricks from chimneys and cracked the courthouse to its foundation. The motion appeared to proceed from south of west to north of east, or the reverse, and was greatest near the larger watercourses. In the shock of December 16 several chimneys were thrown down. At Clarksville, P. H. Cole reported the continuance of the earthquakes to December 15, 1812, one occurring on December 14.

In Christian County, Ky., a fine spring became muddy and remained so for several hours. At the same time it became charged with hydrogen sulphide, presumably from the disturbance of decaying organic matter in the deposits from which it came.

In Arkansas, according to Mr. Hempstead, a delegate to Congress from Missouri Territory, the roads between New Madrid, where court was held, and the settlements of Arkansas, 200 miles distant, were rendered impassible by the earthquake. This made a circuit of 300 miles necessary, seriously interfering with the accessibility to the judiciary.

At St. Genevieve, Dr. Robertson, who then resided there, kept a record of the shocks until they amounted to more than 500, when he became weary of the task.

At St. Louis, according to Mr. Riddick, the first shock was felt about 2.15 a. m. December 16, rousing people from sleep by the motion and the rattling of windows, doors, and furniture, to which was added a peculiar rumbling noise, resembling a number of carriages passing over a pavement. At 2.47, 3.34, daybreak, 8, and 11.30 a. m. other shocks were felt, lasting from a few seconds to 2 minutes. Some chimneys were thrown down and a few stone houses split.

OHIO VALLEY.

At the time of the New Madrid earthquake Cincinnati and Louisville were among the largest settlements west of the Allegheny Mountains and the only large towns near the earthquake center. As would be expected, therefore, it is from these places that the fullest details of the shocks are obtained.

LOUISVILLE.

The record of the shock at Louisville was kept by Jared Brooks and was published by Henry McMurtrie in his sketches of Louisville.[1] Brooks constructed a number of pendulums of different lengths to detect the horizontal movements and a number of springs to show the vertical vibrations. In this manner he was able to note and measure many vibrations not generally felt. His account in the Sketches gives many interesting details regarding the intensities of the shocks and the weather conditions. He also classified the shocks into six groups according to their intensities (see p. 33).

The following table summarizes the shocks as recorded by Brooks in the publication mentioned. It will be found to differ somewhat in totals from the classified table of shocks, page 34, as, in the absence of the assignment of definite intensities in the text, it has not always been possible to determine the strength of a particular shock.

Record of the earthquake shocks at Louisville.[2]

Date.	Hour.	Strength.	Weather.
1811. Dec. 16	2.15 a. m......	Violent.............................	Cloudy and misty; temperature above freezing.
	2.30 a. m......	....do................	Do.
	7.20 a. m......	Strong.......................	Do.
17	5 a. m.........	.....do....................	Cloudy; some rain.
	11.40 a. m.....	Strong to intense................	Do.
18	....	6 considerable shocks..............	Cold; snowing.
19	....	Very slight.....................	Winter weather.

[1] McMurtrie, Henry, Sketches of Louisville and its environs, Louisville, 1819. Appendix.
[2] Compiled from notes of Jared Brooks.

Record of the earthquake shocks at Louisville—Continued.

Date.	Hour.	Strength.	Weather.
1811.			
Dec. 20	10.53 a. m	Considerable	Clear, calm, cold.
	9 p. m	Slight tremors	Warm; overcast.
21	10.48 a. m	....do	Strong west wind.
22–28	8 to 12 a. m	....do	Pleasant, freezing weather; winds west.
	8 to 12 p. m	....do	Do.
29		More frequent tremors	Weather becoming thicker.
30	11 a. m	Considerable	Cloudy; heavy mist; temperature about freezing.
31	4.05 a. m	Strong	Rainy.
	4.45 a. m	Moderate	Do.
1812.			
Jan. 1	12.21 a. m	Considerable	Do.
	9 a. m	Slight	Snowing.
	9 p. m	....do	Light west wind; barely freezing.
2	12.30 a. m	Considerable	Weather clearing.
3	8 to 12 a. m	Strong tremors	Cloudy, cold.
4–8		Slight tremors	Fair, moderate weather; westerly winds.
9	3 a. m	Severe	Cold and pleasant.
		Slight tremors all day	Do.
10	7 p. m	Considerable	Weather becoming overcast.
11	7 a. m	Slight tremors	Foggy.
	9 p. m	....do	Cold; cloudy.
12	9 to 12	....do	Cold; clear to overcast.
13	11 to 12 a. m	Incessant tremors	Fair and cold.
	12 noon	Considerable	Do.
	3 p. m	Slight	Do.
14	11 a. m	....do	Weather thickening.
	Night, a. m	Tremors	Do.
15	11 to 1 noon	Incessant tremors	Hazy; variable wind.
16		Very faint tremors	Pleasant; turning cloudy.
17	9 p. m	Slight	Snowing.
18	11 a. m	Considerable	Rainy, lightning, foggy.
19		No shocks reported	Unsettled.
20	Night, a. m	Very slight tremors	Cold; some snow.
21		Slight tremors	Very cold, hazy, damp.
22	Day	Considerable shocks	Damp and foggy, but cold.
23	8.50 a. m	Very violent	Hazy; south wind.
	1 p. m	Considerable	Rainy, hail, snow.
	10.30 p. m	....do	Do.
24	Morning	....do	Rain and sleet; foggy.
	11 to 12 a. m	Slight	Do.
	10.30 p. m	Severe	Rainy.
25		Tremors	Cold, gloomy, foggy.
26		Slight tremors	Calm, overcast, dryer.
27	Morning	Strong tremor	Cold, calm, overcast.
	8.50 a. m	Violent	Very quiet; almost fair.
28	9 to 12 a. m	Frequent vibrations	Sunny weather.
	9 p. m	Slight tremor	Warm, misty, overcast.
29	9 to 11 a. m	Incessant slight tremors	Rain in morning; overcast.
	11.30 a. m	Considerable	Do.
30	9 to 12 a. m	Barely perceptible	Unsettled weather.
	3 p. m	Strong tremor	Clearing.
31	9 to 12 a. m	Continual tremor	Sun shining dimly.
	P. m	Considerable tremors	Do.
Feb. 1	9 a. m. to 1 p. m	Tremors and vibrations	Do.
2	2 a. m	Considerable shock	Calm, hazy.
	9 to 12 a. m	Less than usual	Partly cloudy.
	12 to 10 p. m	Slight motion	Do.
	10.45 p. m	Considerable shock	Rainy.
	10.45 to 11.30 p. m	Frequent slight tremors	Do.
3	12.36 a. m	Considerable motion	Do.
	6 a. m	Slight tremor	Do.
	8 to 12 a. m	Moderate tremors	Clearing weather; windy.
	2 p. m	Slight shock	Do.
4	A. m	No shocks	Clear and pleasant.
	3.30 p. m	Tremors begin	Sky suddenly overcast at 2 p. m.
	4.30 p. m	Violent	Sprinkle of rain.
5	8.30 a. m	Moderate shock	Cold and fair.
	11.15 a. m	Strong, vertical vibrations	Do.
	1.45 p. m	Moderate shock	Do.
	2.37 p. m	Severe	Do.
	4.48 p. m	....do	Do.
6	Night, a. m	Slight tremors	Do.
	8.30 p. m	Heavy shock	Cold, calm, hazy.
7	3.15 a. m	Tremendous	Do.
	3.15 to 5 a. m	Constant motion	Do.
	5 to 12 a. m	Frequent jarrings	Cloudy.
	12 to 8 p. m	Tremors every 10 minutes on average.	Rain and snow after 2 p. m.

Record of the earthquake shocks at Louisville—Continued.

Date.		Hour.	Strength.	Weather.
1812. Feb.	7	8.10 p. m......	Severe......................	Stormy.
		10.10 p. m....	Severe to tremendous...............	Do.
	8	12.05 a. m....	Moderate shock..................	Cloudy.
		12 to 6 a. m....	Many tremors......................	Cloudy, or hazy.
		9.25 p. m......	Moderate shock.............	Overcast.
	9	8.45 a. m......	Smart shock................	Clear and pleasant.
		3.48 p. m......	....do...........	Do.
		4.10 p. m......	Frequent slight shocks...........	Do.
	10	9.08 a. m......	Slight shocks....................	Overcast.
		10.13 a. m......	....do........	Do.
		10.30 a. m......	....do........	Do.
		11 a. m........	Pendulums all in motion............	Thunder shower.
		11.50 a. m....	Largely vertical motion............	Calm and rainy.
		3 p. m........	Smart shock................	Partly cloudy.
		8.25 p. m......	Single hard shove.............	Do.
	11	5.40 a. m......	Faint shock................	Do.
		6 a. m........	Slight motions...............	Do.
		10 a. m........	....do........	Do.
		12 m..........	Considerable shock.............	Pleasant.
	12	9 to 12 a. m....	Several tremors...............	Do.
	13	12 to 6 a. m....	....do........	Cloudy.
		9.19 a. m......	Considerable tremor.............	Do.
		10 to 11 a. m ..	Several tremors; slight.........	Do.
		12 m..........	Faint shock................	Do.
	14	10 to 11 a. m...	Several faint tremors.............	Rainy.
		2.09 p. m......	All pendulums moved............	Clearing.
		12.30 a. m....	Considerable tremor.............	Fair.
	15	11.20 a. m....	Slight tremor................	Cloudy.
		12.30 p. m....	....do........	Do.
		3 p. m........	....do........	Partly cloudy.
	16	9.15 a. m to 12 a. m.	Continual tremor..............	Rainy.
		12 m..........	Considerable motion..............	Do.
		10 p. m........	Considerable shock.............	Overcast.
	17	4 a. m........	Shock of some strength............	Pleasant.
		11 to 12 a. m...	Continual tremor..............	Do.
		3.07 p. m......	Slight shock..............	Do.
	18	2 p. m........	Motion considerable (over 70 tremors during day and night).	Fair.
	19	8 to 10 a. m...	Pendulums swing half the time.....	Fine weather.
	20	Night, a. m...	Tremors; few shocks during day....	Cloudy.
		10 p. m........	Moderate shock................	Do.
		11.50 p. m.....	....do.....	Do.
	21	Night, a. m...	Frequent slight vibrations.........	Do.
		11.30 to 12 a. m.	Pendulums in motion.............	Do.
		8 p. m........	....do.......	Do.
	22	9 a. m........	Perceptible motion..................	Do.
		P. m..........	Frequent slight movements..........	Rainy.
		12 p. m........	Somewhat alarming shock..........	Do.
	23	8 to 12 a. m ...	Frequent tremors.............	Do.
		12 m..........	Considerable tremor..........	Do.
		4 p. m........	Smart vibration	Do.
		8.30 p. m......	Strong vibration	Do.
		12 p. m........	....do......	Do.
	24	9 a. m........	4-inch pendulum in motion (little motion through day).	Cloudy.
	25	Sunrise.......	Considerable tremor..............	Fair.
		9 a. m........	Some motion............	Do.
		P. m..........	Pendulums generally at rest........	Do.
	26	10.30 a. m.....	All pendulums in motion........	Do.
		P. m..........	Little motion after sunset..........	Do.
	27	8 to 10 a. m ..	Irregular movements of pendulums .	Do.
		Sunset........	Slight shock (no motion during afternoon).	Do.
	28	4 a. m.........	Moderate shock............	Do.
		10 to 10.30 a. m.	Slight to considerable motion.......	Do.
		1 p. m........	Considerable shock................	Do.
	29	Night, a. m...	Smart motion.................	Do.
		8 a. m........	Sensible shock..............	Do.
		9.30 a. m......	Considerable shock; considerable vertical motion.	Do.
		9.30 a. m. to 1.30 p. m.	Tremors......................	Do.
		6 to 7 p. m....	Pendulums in motion...........	Do.
Mar.	1	9 a. m........	Pendulums move slightly..........	Especially fine weather.
		2 p. m........	Slight motion; stillest day yet as regards shocks.	Do.
	2	2.35 to 3.30 p. m.	Pendulums in motion; noticeable vibrations.	Do.
		8.35 p. m......	Pendulums vibrate strongly........	Do.
	3	Sunrise.......	Smart shock....................	Pleasant.
		8.35 a. m......	Strong shove and much motion.....	Do.
		2 p. m........	Slight shock..................	Do.
		3.30 p. m......	Very slight shock.................	Do.

Record of the earthquake shocks at Louisville—Continued.

Date.	Hour.	Strength.	Weather.
1812. Mar. 4	Sunrise.......	Shock generally felt...............	Pleasant.
	10.30 a. m.....	Sudden long easy shove.............	Overcast.
	5.25 p. m......	Considerable motion................	Cloudy.
	Evening......	Slight motions.....................	Rainy.
5	Sunrise.......	Shock generally felt...............	Do.
	10.36 a. m.....	A considerable shove...............	Dark, cloudy, oppressive.
	12 m..........	Very faint motion..................	Cloudy.
	3 p. m........	Considerable horizontal and perpendicular motion.	Partly cloudy.
6	3 a. m........	Gentle shove.......................	Do.
	11 a. m. to 2 p. m.	Barely perceptible vibration........	Do.
	3 p. m........	....do............................	Do.
	7.35 p. m......	Shock generally felt...............	Do.
7	8 a. m........	Slight but frequent tremors........	Cloudy.
	11 a. m........	Pendulums vibrate considerably; considerable perpendicular motion.	Do.
8	8.30 to 9 a. m..	Short pendulums move slightly.....	Fair.
	9.36 a. m......	Shock generally felt...............	Cloudy.
	Noon..........	Perceptible shock..................	Partly cloudy.
	8 p. m........	Faint tremor.......................	Do.
	9 p. m........	Pendulums in motion...............	Do.
9	Daybreak.....	Perceptible shock..................	Hazy.
	7 to 12 a. m ...	Pendulums in motion at short intervals.	Pleasant.
	12 to 5 p. m...	....do............................	Do.
10	Morning......	3 moderate shoves.................	Fair.
	6 to 9 a. m	Pendulums seldom still.............	Do.
	10.25 a. m.....	Pendulums in motion...............	Do.
	Noon..........	All pendulums in motion...........	Do.
	3.20 p. m......	Several pendulums in motion.......	Do.
	7.20 p. m......	Powerful shoves in one direction....	Overcast.
11	Night, a. m...	2 or 3 movements..................	Cloudy.
	9.20 a. m......	Strong shoves.....................	Do.
	10 a. m........	3 to 6 inch pendulums in motion....	Do.
	12.25 p. m.....	Short pendulum vibrates; little motion in afternoon.	Do.
12	Night, a. m...	Generally felt in town and country..	Approaching fair.
	6.50 a. m......	Short pendulums in motion.........	Do.
	7.08 a. m......	All pendulums in motion...........	Do.
	8.20 to 12 a. m.	Short pendulums in motion most of time.	Do.
	6.30 p. m......	Barely perceptible vertical motion ..	Do.
	8 p. m........	....do............................	Do.
13	Forenoon.....	No vibrations.....................	Do.
14	2 to 3 p. m....	Considerable shock; alarmed people.	Do.
	10.40 a. m. to 1 p. m.	Medium-length pendulums in motion.	Fair.
	9 p. m........	Slight motion.....................	Do.
15	....	Motion similar to preceding day....	Rain and thunder.
16	9 to 10 a. m ...	3-inch vibrator in motion...........	Rainy.
17	9 a. m........	....do............................	Cloudy.
18	8 to 10 a. m ...	Vibrators and pendulums in motion.	Fine weather.
	Evening......	The same during day and evening at intervals.	Do.
19	8.10 to 12 a. m.	Pendulums in motion...............	Fair.
	Afternoon.....	Frequent slight motions............	Do.
	Sunset........	2 slight shocks....................	Overcast.
20	8 a. m........	6-inch pendulum in motion.........	Hazy sun.
	9.20 to 12 a. m.	Pendulum swings constantly.......	Do.
21	11.35 a. m. to 6 p. m.	Shorter vibrations; nearly constant.	Rainy.
	12 p. m.......	Strong shock.....................	Do.
22	8.25 a. m......	6-inch pendulum moved considerably.	Snowing.
	10.05 to 11 a. m.	All pendulums in motion..........	Snowing occasionally.
	3 p. m........	....do............................	Do.
23	11.25 a. m.....	2 and 4 inch pendulums vibrate.....	Calm, cloudy.
	2 p. m........	Similar to preceding..............	Hazy sun.
	12 p. m.......	Considerable shock................	Overcast, foggy.
24	7.20 a. m......	Similar to previous morning.......	Do.
25	7 to 8 a. m	Less than previous day............	Hazy sun.
26	A. m..........	Still decreasing...................	Do.
	P. m..........	No vibrations.....................	Rainy.
27	A. m..........	....do............................	Rain and lightning.
	2.20 to 7.10 p. m	Pendulums vibrate.................	Rain or snow.
28	....	Only short pendulums move........	Fair.
29	7.30 a. m......	Perceptible shock..................	Fair and frosty.
30	....	Pendulum vibrations...............	Do.
31	....	Least motion of any day...........	Clear and crisp.
Apr. 1	....	Several shocks sufficient to move 4-inch pendulum; 1 in night felt by people.	Hazy sun.

Record of the earthquake shocks at Louisville—Continued.

Date.	Hour.	Strength.	Weather.
1812. Apr. 2	....	Similar to Apr. 1..................	Dim sun.
3	11 a. m........	Sensible shock...............	Fair.
4	....	Very slight tremors..............	Fair to overcast.
5	....	Vibrations barely perceptible by pendulums.	Cloudy and gloomy.
6	Sunrise to 2 p. m.	Frequent vibrations of shorter pendulums.	Looked like gathering storm.
7	....	Motion at sunrise with slight vibrations all day.	Overcast, unsettled.
8	6 a. m........	Perceptible shock................	Overcast, very dark.
	3 p. m........	Moderate shock..............	Overcast.
	P. m..........	Pendulums move at sunset........	Do.
9	A. m..........	Very slight movements of pendulums in morning.	Partly cloudy.
10	11 a. m.......	Perceptible shock...............	Cloudy, some rain.
11	8 a. m........	Pendulums in motion...........	Overcast, windy.
12	....	Very slight movements...........	Overcast, but little wind.
13	9 a. m........	.....do...................	Overcast.
14	....	.....do...................	Do.
15	....	.....do...................	Do.
16	....	.....do...................	Do.
17	....	Perceptible shock at daylight......	Rainy.
18	....	Pendulums in frequent action......	Heavy thunder storms.
19	....	.....do...................	Rain and thunder.
20	....	Slight motion..................	Showers.
21	....	.....do...................	Do.
22	6 to 10 a. m ...	Considerable motion............	Fair.
	10 p. m.......	.....do...................	Do.
23-27	....	Movements each day; generally slight, but some stronger.	Fair and dry but with some haze.
28	A. m..........	Perceptible shock before daybreak ..	Calm, warm.
	7 to 10 a. m ...	Strong vibrations..............	Do.
	P. m..........	Strong vibrations in evening.......	Do.
29	....	Motion moderate in morning, weak at night.	Dry and calm; thunder shower in evening.
30	....	Pendulums vibrate morning and evening.	Showers and thunder.
May 1	....	Many perceptible shocks; pendulums constantly in motion.	Rainy.
2	8 a. m........	Pendulums in motion...........	Do.
3	....	Pendulums in motion morning and evening.	Do.
4	8 a. m........	Pendulums in motion..........	Threatening weather.
	10.25 a. m....	Moderate to severe............	Do.
5	7.10 a. m.....	Frequent vibrations...........	Fine weather.

CINCINNATI.

A detailed account of the earthquake of 1811–12 as observed at Cincinnati is presented by Drake, who in fact left the only scientific record of the shocks at this point which the writer has seen.[1] The chronological list of the disturbances was given in the table on pages 19–20. Of the first shock he says:

At 24 minutes past 2 o'clock a. m. mean time the first shock occurred. The motion was a quick oscillation or rocking, by most persons believed to be west and east; by some south and north. Its continuance, taking the average of all the observations I could collect, was 6 or 7 minutes. Several persons assert that it was preceded by a rumbling or rushing noise; but this is denied by others, who were awake at the commencement. It was so violent as to agitate the loose furniture of our rooms, open partition doors that were fastened with falling latches, and throw off the tops of a few chimneys in the vicinity of the town. It seems to have been stronger in the valley of the Ohio than in the adjoining uplands. Many families living on the elevated ridges of Kentucky, not more than 20 miles from the river, slept during the shock; which can not be said, perhaps, of any family in town.

---

[1] Drake, Daniel, Natural and statistical view or pictures of Cincinnati, Cincinnati, 1815, pp. 233–244.

Of the severe shock of January 23 he says:

About 9 o'clock a. m. a great number of strong undulations occurred in quick succession. They continued 4 or 5 minutes, having two or three distinct exascerbations during that time. An instrument constructed on the principle of that used in Naples, at the time of the memorable Calabrian earthquakes, marked the direction of the undulations from south-southeast to north-northwest. This earthquake was nearly equal to that which commenced the series on the 16th ultimo.

His account of the severe shock of February 7 is as follows:

At 45 minutes past 3 o'clock a. m. several alarming shocks in rapid succession. The instrument already mentioned indicated the three principal heaves to be from the southwest, the south-southwest, and south-southeast. The last greatly surpassed any other undulation ever known at this place. It threw down the tops of more chimneys, made wider fissures in the brick walls, and produced vertigo and nausea in a greater number of people, than the earthquakes of either the 16th of December or the 23d of January. It was said by some that this earthquake was preceded by a light and a noise; but this was denied by others, who were awake and collected in mind and senses.

On February 8 the following occurred:

At 40 minutes past 10 o'clock a shock considerably stronger than either of the preceding [of February 8]. It was observed to produce in suspended and elevated bodies a very sensible degree of trembling, but no oscillation; indicating, perhaps, a vertical instead of the horizontal motion of the previous shocks. Immediately before this shock I had the satisfaction of hearing, for the first time, a noise such as preceded, according to the report of some of our citizens, most of the principal earthquakes. It was a peculiar, faint, dull, rumbling or rushing sound, near the horizon, to the southwest. It seemed to approach but not arrive at the place of observation, and after continuing four or five seconds was succeeded by the shake. During the remainder of the night and the next day the earth was in the same state of tremor which it suffered on the 5th and 6th.

Discussing the intensities of the shocks, Drake adds:

The violence of different earthquakes is best indicated by their efficiency in altering the structure of the more superficial parts of the earth, and in agitating, subverting, or destroying the bodies which they support. On a comparative scale, formed from such remarks, at this place the first shock of the 16th of December, 1811, that of the 23d of January, 1812, and the first on the 7th of February, occupy, above the rest, a decided elevation, and constitute the first class. To the second class belong the shock at 20 minutes past 7 o'clock a. m., December 16, that on the 27th of January, and that at 40 minutes past 10 o'clock p. m. on the 8th of February. Of the remainder, one-half, by estimation, may be referred to a fourth class, composed of those which were felt only by persons not in action; and the remainder will constitute a third class of intermediate violence. The numerous tremors and ebullitions that were detected by pendulums, and the delicate sensations of a few nice observers, when at perfect rest, may constitute the fifth and lowest order of these multiplied agitations.

After giving the description quoted above, Drake presents a detailed account of the physical phenomena observed during this period of disturbance and during previous earthquakes. (See p. 13.)

OTHER LOCALITIES.

At Jeffersonville, opposite Louisville, the shocks were felt very much as they were in Louisville. At Red Bank, 150 miles below

Louisville, Anthony New stated that from December 16, 1811, to January 4, 1812, there were 20 to 30 shocks, the one shortly after 2 a. m. and the one at sunrise on the 16th being the most violent. These shocks, which cracked or threw down many chimneys and caused the people to flee from their houses, are said to have been accompanied by a noise coming from the west. At Vincennes, on the Wabash River in Indiana, the first shock was very severe, menacing the safety of the houses, and was followed by shocks of less violence for several days. At Lebanon, Ohio, the vibrations, which appeared to move from east to west, were so great that the houses were vacated. At Circleville, in the same State, a violent trembling sufficient to bring persons from their beds was experienced at the time of the first shock, while a lesser shock was felt at 8 a. m. In the Green River region and Henderson County, Ky., the first shock, which was alarming in its nature, was followed through night and day up to December 30 by less violent shocks. On the latter date a shock more severe than any of those preceding was experienced, overturning nearly every chimney in Henderson County. The shock of 4 a. m., February 7, was severe at Pittsburgh, being greater than any previously experienced. Many persons left their houses.

GREAT LAKES REGION.

Judge James Witherall, writing from Detroit, Mich., reported that the first shocks were distinctly felt in that region. The weather was cold but calm. In February, 1812, he wrote that the earthquakes still continued.

On the 3d instant, 14 minutes past 4 p. m., a small shock was felt; the mercury low, but not quite in the ball; it had risen very considerably a few hours previous to the shock. On the 7th, at 4 p. m., the weather continuing moderate, the shock was strong, nearly equaling the one I previously mentioned to you, and continued about 90 seconds; on the same evening at half-past 7 another small shock; at 55 minutes past 9 the same evening another small shock; at 11, another; and at 12 a. m. of the 8th, one which seemed to produce a different motion, that is, like pounding up and down instead of oscillating.

A. B. Woodward, another judge in Michigan Territory, wrote on April 7:

We have had nine shocks of the earthquake here, of which I have an exact memorandum of eight and have somehow entirely lost the time of the other. I felt four myself. I know only one person, a French lady, who felt the whole; speaking here of the eight.

In a letter dated June 23, the same gentleman observes:

In a late journey to the Rivière aux Tranches, in upper Canada, I found the number of shocks of the earthquake felt there was exactly the same as here—that is, nine.

ATLANTIC COASTAL AND PIEDMONT PLAINS.

The shocks were distinctly felt throughout the Piedmont and Coastal plains from Washington southward, but were not very noticeable farther north, although reported at Baltimore and even at Boston. The nontransmission of the shocks in the Northern States was probably due in part to their distance from the centrum and in part to the oblique angle made by the line of transmission of the vibrations to the strike of the rock strata, the shock apparently being transmitted much more readily in directions at right angles to the trend of the strata, as in the southern Appalachians, than in those making very low angles, as at the northern end of the system. The following include the principal allusions found in regard to the shocks.[1]

Washington.—On the morning of Monday, the 16 December, 1811, several shocks of earthquakes were felt at the city of Washington. The first of these happened at 3 o'clock, and in some houses was considerable, enough to shake the doors and windows and wake persons from their sleep. There were successive tremors. Tassels of curtains were seen to move, and pitchers of washing stands were heard to rattle upon their basins. The sound was very distinguishable and was believed by many to pass from southwest to northeast. The alarm was so great in some families that searches were made from room to room to discover the robbers who were imagined to have broken into the houses.

A second shock, though lighter, was experienced about 6 o'clock, and a third about 8.

A gentleman standing in his chamber at his desk and writing, in the third story of a brick house upon the Capitol Hill, suddenly perceived his body to be in motion, vibrating backward and forward and producing dizziness. Not suspecting at the moment that the uncomfortable sensation was caused by an earthquake, he examined his desk to know whether it stood firm. Finding that it did, he dropped his pen and, turning his eyes upward, discerned that the looking-glass and other things hanging near him were in a similar motion.

Another person was near a table placed beneath a mirror. Feeling a giddiness come upon him, he seized the table for support. The general agitation of the chamber and house ceased in about a minute; but the looking-glass, which was suspended in the usual manner, continued to swing for some seconds longer.

Points in the South.—In Richmond the signs of an earthquake were witnessed by many persons. At 3 o'clock on the same morning (the 16th of December) there were said to be three successive shocks, another about 6, and a third about 8. Several people were impressed with a belief that thieves had entered their dwellings, and in one of the most elevated mansions the bells were set a-ringing in both the upper and lower rooms. The noise and concussion were supposed by some to proceed from east to west. It was stated at Norfolk that two very distinct shocks were felt in that town and in Portsmouth, to wit, at 3 and 8 o'clock in the morning of the 16th. Some clocks were reported to have stopped, the doors rattled, and articles hanging from the ceilings of shops and houses swung to and fro, although a perfect calm prevailed.

At Raleigh, N. C., several slight earthquakes were felt on the morning of the 16th of December. The first happened between 2 and 3 o'clock and was distinctly perceived by all who were awake at the time. Two others were reported to have occurred between that time and 7 o'clock, but were not plainly observed except by some members of the legislature who were in the Statehouse and were considerably alarmed at the shaking of the building.

---

[1] Mitchill, S. L., Trans. Lit. and Philos. Soc. New York, vol. 1, 1815, pp. 281-307.

From Georgetown, S. C., it was told that several shocks had been experienced between the hours of 3 and 8 on the morning of the 16th. The inhabitants were much alarmed. The shocks were so considerable that the parade ground of the fort was said to have settled from 1 to 2 inches below its former level. A tub of water standing upon a table in the barracks was reported to have been overset by the jarring of the building. Another severe shock was felt two days afterwards at noon.

At Columbia, S. C., the inhabitants were alarmed by repeated shocks. The first took place at half after 2 in the morning of Monday, which was represented as shaking the houses as if rocked by the waves of the sea. It was followed after the cessation of a minute by three slighter ones. At 8 o'clock two others took place, and at 10 some slight ones. The South Carolina College appeared to rock from its foundation and a part of its plaster fell, which so alarmed the students that they left their chambers without their clothes. It seemed as if all the buildings would be leveled. The dogs barked, fowls made a racket, and many persons ran about with lights, not knowing where to go so great was their terror. During the first agitation it was observed that the air felt as if impregnated with a vapor, which lasted for some time.

At Charleston, S. C., the sensation was of considerable strength. One account stated that on the morning of the 16th, at a few minutes before 3 o'clock, a severe shock of an earthquake was felt. Its duration conjectured to have been between 2 and 3 minutes. For an hour previous, though the air was perfectly calm and several stars visible, there was at intervals of about 5 minutes a rumbling noise like that of distant thunder, which increased in violence of sound just before the shock was felt. The vibration of St. Philip's steeple caused the clock bell to ring about 10 seconds. Two other shocks were felt afterwards, one a little before 8, and the other about a quarter of an hour after. Both these were slighter and shorter than the first. Many of the family clocks were stopped by the concussions. In many wells the water was considerably agitated. From another source it was related that Charleston was shaken by an earthquake severely at the time before specified. This was preceded by a noise resembling the blowing of a smith's bellows. The agitation of the earth was such that the bells in the church steeples rang to a degree indicative of an alarm of fire. The houses were so much moved that many persons were induced to rise from their beds. The clocks generally stopped. Another slight shock was experienced about 15 minutes after, and yet another at 8 o'clock. This last one produced a considerable rattling among glass, china, and other furniture. A looking-glass hanging against a west wall was observed to vibrate 2 or 3 inches from north to south.

The inhabitants of Savannah were sensible of four earthquakes. The first was on the morning of the 16th of December between 2 and 3 o'clock. It was preceded by a flash of light and a rattling noise resembling that of a carriage passing over a paved road. It lasted about a minute. A second soon succeeded, but its duration was shorter. A third happened about 8 o'clock, and a fourth about noon on the 17th. Persons who experienced the hardest shock were made to totter as if on shipboard. Its course was believed to be from southwest to northeast.

It was observed by Dr. Macbride, of Pineville, S. C., that the earthquake terrified the inhabitants exceedingly. It was accompanied by several appearances that countenance the theory of this phenomenon which brings in the agency of the electric fluid. (1) The infrequency or absence of thunder storms; that is, they were much less frequent this year than usual, especially in the autumn. (2) Immediately before the earthquake a red appearance of the clouds which had much darkened the water for 24 hours immediately before the shock. (3) The loudness of the thunder, and the number of the peals within 24 hours after the first shock and but a few hours before the last, which was felt before he wrote. Such thunder was very unusual at that season.

The Hon. Israel Pickens, of Buncombe County, N. C., received a letter from the Rev. John Carrigan, dated the 28th of February, and containing the following information:

"During my travels lately to and from the State of Georgia I made it a part of my business to obtain the most accurate accounts of the present shaking of the earth from all parts. I have found that in all parts of the Continent the motion of the earth has been the same and its partiality remarked in the same neighborhoods. In this country the first rocking (as it is generally called) was perceived on the 23d of December, a little before daylight. Since that time it has been observed almost every week through South Carolina and parts of Georgia. Several persons in those States have told me that they have felt it almost every day since. No damages have arisen more than a few bricks shaken off some chimneys. There is no truth in the report in circulation respecting the fall of the Painted Rock and other extraordinaries in Buncombe County. I gave my friend, Col. Freeman, in Georgia, a call, who informed me that he had particularly noticed some tall poplars in his lane during the time of the second shock rocking with an equable motion from northeast to southwest, which I have found to be general. On the 7th and 16th instant the shaking has been general here."

NATURE OF THE VIBRATIONS.

In the New Madrid area proper the only evidence of the nature of the vibrations is the accounts of those persons who experienced them. Of these Bringier, who experienced one of the major shocks, describes the action as a blowing up of the earth accompanied by loud explosions.[1] Casseday writes:[2] "It seems as if the surface of the earth was afloat and set in motion by a slight application of immense power, but when this regularity is broken by a sudden cross shove, all order is destroyed, and a boiling action is produced, during the continuance of which the degree of violence is greatest, and the scene most dreadful."

Others described the movement as an "undulation of the earth resembling waves, increasing in elevation as they advanced, and when they had attained a certain fearful height the earth would burst."[3]

Le Sieur likewise says: "The earth was observed to roll in waves a few feet high with visible depressions between. By and by these swells burst throwing up large volumes of water, sand, and coal."[4] Haywood writes that in Tennessee the motions were undulating, the agitated surfaces "quivering like the flesh of a beef just killed." The motion is said to have "progressed from west to east and was sometimes, though seldom, perpendicular, resembling a house raised and suddenly let fall to the ground."[5]

Audubon, who experienced one of the shocks while riding in Kentucky, says that "the ground rose and fell in successive furrows like the ruffled waters of a lake. * * * The earth waved like a field of corn before the breeze."[6]

There were great differences in the intensity and destructiveness of the shocks. According to Foster:[7] "Sometimes they would come

[1] Bringier, L., Am. Jour. Sci., 1st ser., vol. 3, 1821, pp. 15-46.

[2] Casseday Ben., History of Louisville, 1852, p. 122.

[3] Flint, Timothy, Recollections of the last ten years, Boston, 1826, p. 223.

[4] Le Sieur, Godfrey, quoted in Am. Geologist, vol. 30, 1902, p. 80.

[5] Haywood, John, Natural and aboriginal history of Tennessee, Nashville, 1823, p. 124.

[6] Audubon, J. J., Audubon and his Journals, New York, 1897, vol. 2, pp. 234-237.

[7] Foster, J. W., The Mississippi Valley, Chicago, 1869, p. 20.

on gradually and finally culminate; again they would come without premonition and in terrific force and gradually subside." When the shocks were severe it was practically impossible to stand. Bradbury and his crew, who encountered one of the severe shocks while on shore caring for his boat, had great difficulty in preventing themselves from being thrown down, and one of the party was nearly precipitated into the river.[1] Again Flint says that when the shocks "were at the severest point of their motion the people were thrown on the ground at almost every step. A French gentleman told me that in escaping from his house, the largest in the village, he found he had left an infant behind, and he attempted to mount up the raised piazza to recover the child and was thrown down a dozen times in succession."[2]

Vertical shocks do not appear to have been lacking in the New Madrid area, but, according to Flint, were less destructive than the horizontal type. He says: "The shocks were clearly distinguishable into two classes, those in which the motion was horizontal and those in which it was perpendicular. The latter were attended with the explosions and the terrible mixture of noises, * * * but they were by no means as destructive as the other."[3]

In the more remote districts the action was less intense, producing only vibrations and tremors. There appears, however, to have been more or less of surface movements, as the shocks were much more distinctly felt by those living in the alluvial flats of the valleys than by those on the rock uplands, notwithstanding that it is only through the rocks that the shocks could be transmitted to the distances observed. The slight vibrations in the latter must, therefore, have been greatly magnified on transmission to the alluvial masses. The intensities in valley and upland differed sufficiently to be noticeable at the time. Drake, speaking of Cincinnati, says:[4] "The convulsion was greater along the Mississippi, as well as along the Ohio, than in the uplands. The strata in both valleys are loose. The more tenacious layers of clay and loam spread over the adjoining hills, many of which are composed of horizontal limestone, suffered but little derangement."

At Louisville Jared Brooks constructed a number of pendulums varying from 1 to 6 inches in length. According to his records, as presented in McMurtrie's history,[5] although there was great variation in the rapidity and amplitude of the vibrations at different times, there was often considerable uniformity during a single shock. Sometimes when the amplitude was short only the 1 or 2 inch pendulums would vibrate. At other times the 3 and 4 inch pendulums

[1] Bradbury, John, Early western travels, Cleveland, 1904, vol. 5, p. 257.
[2] Flint, Timothy, op. cit., p. 225.
[3] Op. cit., p. 224.
[4] Drake, Daniel, Natural and statistical view or picture of Cincinnati, Cincinnati, 1815, p. 235.
[5] McMurtrie, H., Sketches of Louisville and its environs, Louisville, 1819, Appendix.

would move while both the longer and shorter ones remained stationary, and again the 6-inch pendulum alone would be in motion. The great majority of the vibrations at Louisville appear to have been horizontal and to have varied from mere tremors to strong movements to and fro. Usually a considerable number of movements occurred during each shock, but at times the motion was like a shove in a single direction without any corresponding movement in the opposite direction. Sometimes two or three such shoves occurred in succession, varying in intensity from gentle to sharp. A few motions were vertical and were recorded only by the spring indicators, the pendulums remaining quiet. Other notes on the movements are given on pages 22 to 26.

CLASSIFICATION OF INTENSITIES.

No record of intensities was kept at New Madrid or vicinity, but at Louisville, only a short distance away, a systematic record was kept by Jared Brooks, who divided the shocks into six classes, viz:

First rate. Most tremendous, so as to threaten the destruction of the town, and which would soon effect it should the action continue with the same degree of violence; buildings oscillate largely and irregularly and grind against each other; the walls split and begin to yield; chimneys, parapets, and gable ends break in various directions and topple to the ground.

Second rate. Less violent but very severe.

Third rate. Moderate but alarming to people generally.

Fourth rate. Perceptible to the feeling of those who are still and not subject to other motion or sort of jarring that may resemble this.

[Fifth rate. Not defined.]

Sixth rate. Although often causing a strange sort of sensation, absence, and sometimes giddiness, the motion is not to be ascertained positively, but by the vibrators or other objects placed for that purpose.

In his classified list he records a total of 1,874 shocks between December 16, 1811, and March 15, 1812, but many more occurred in the succeeding months for over a year, as shown in the tables on pages 25–26. Of the 1,874 shocks, 8 are classed as violent, 10 as very severe, 35 moderate, 65 generally perceptible, 89 of "fifth rate," and 1,667 indistinctly felt or noted by movements of delicately poised objects. (See table on p. 34.)

PERIODS OF ACTIVITY.

The greatest intensity of action occurred not at the beginning of the disturbances but in the first half of the following February and continued through the later part of February and the early part of March. The activity beginning on December 16 gradually increased until the middle of January, but fell off during the later part of the month until only a little over one-third of the former number of shocks was felt. Then followed a second period of great activity in late January and early February and after a falling off in the middle of the month a period of still greater activity late in February. After another falling off in early March a further period of intensity developed about the middle of the month. This is brought out by the lines in figure 2.

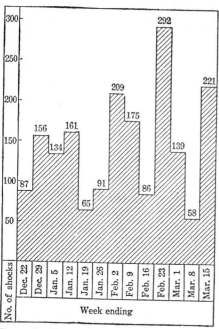

FIGURE 2.—Diagram showing earthquake activity by weeks, based on Brooks's summary of shocks at Louisville, Ky.

Figure 3 shows similar lines for shocks of the first, second, third, and fourth intensities. It is interesting to note that the lines for the heavy shocks, or those of intensities from 1 to 3, are synchronous, but that of the fourth intensity tends to be highest when the others are relatively low. This suggests that instead of readjustments by a few large slips (intensities 1, 2, and 3) the change is at times by a large number of small slips, giving rise to very faint shocks, such as those of intensity 4. Shocks in the weeks ending December 22 and February 9 furnish examples of readjustment by a few large slips, while those of January 12 and March 8 show perhaps equally large readjustments by a considerable number of small slips.

The number and intensities of earthquake shocks from December 16 to March 15 are brought out in the following table of Brooks:

Distribution and intensities of the shocks of the New Madrid earthquake.

End of week.	Rate.						Total.
	First.	Second.	Third.	Fourth.	Fifth.	Sixth.	
Dec. 22	3	2	3	1	12	66	87
29					6	150	156
Jan. 5		1		9	3	119	134
12		1		10		150	161
19				4	6	55	65
26	1	1	7	2	2	78	91
Feb. 2	1		4	6	7	191	209
9	3	5	7	5	15	140	175
16			3	6	12	65	86
23			4	6	4	278	292
Mar. 1			1	4	8	126	139
8			2	9	8	39	58
15			2	3	6	210	221
	8	10	35	65	89	1,667	1,874

RELATION OF DISTRIBUTION OF SHOCKS TO TIME OF DAY.

For the purpose of determining the relation of distribution to time of day, about 178 shocks, the hours of which were more or less specifically stated, were selected from the list of Brooks (see table, pp. 22 to 26) and grouped in the table given on page 36, which shows the number of shocks of five grades of intensity occurring in each hour of the day. It will be noted that of the minor

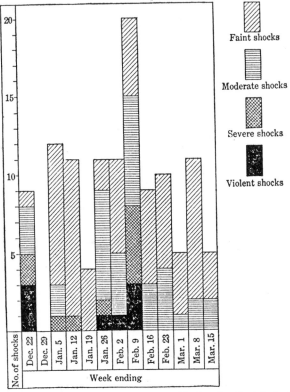

FIGURE 3.—Diagram showing earthquake activity by intensities, based on Brooks's summary of shocks at Louisville.

shocks very few are recorded in the night, doubtless because they were not of sufficient strength to awaken sleepers. Beginning at 6 a. m. there is, according to the tables, a gradual increase of activity to a time between 9 and 11, after which it falls off until 1 o'clock, at which hour almost no shocks are recorded. A second but lesser period of intensity develops about 3, with a falling off from 4 to 7, after which the intensity increases again from 8 to 11. Between 11 and 12 only 1 shock is recorded, but considerable activity is manifest between 12 and 1 in the night. (See fig. 4.)

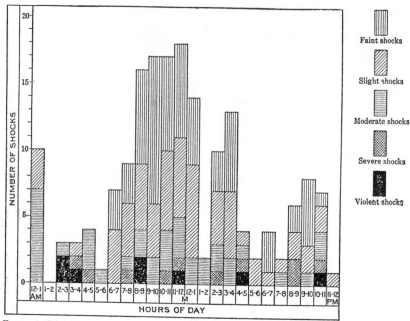

FIGURE 4.—Diagram showing earthquake activity by hours of the day, based on 178 shocks whose time of occurrence was recorded.

Distribution of shocks with reference to time of day.

Hour.	Violent shocks.	Severe shocks.	Moderate shocks.	Slight shocks; strong vibrations.	Faint shocks; tremors.	Total.
12 to 1 a. m						
1 to 2 a. m			7	3		10
2 to 3 a. m	2		1			3
3 to 4 a. m	1	1		1		3
4 to 5 a. m		1	3			4
5 to 6 a. m			1			1
6 to 7 a. m				4	3	7
7 to 8 a. m		1	1	4	3	9
8 to 9 a. m	2		2	5	7	16
9 to 10 a. m			2	4	11	17
10 to 11 a. m	1	1	3	6	7	17
11 to 12 m		1	3	6	7	18
12 m. to 1 p. m			2	7	5	14
1 to 2 p. m			2			2
2 to 3 p. m		1	2	4	3	10
3 to 4 p. m	1	1	1	5	6	13
4 to 5 p. m				1		4
5 to 6 p. m				2		2
6 to 7 p. m			1	1	3	4
7 to 8 p. m		2		1		2
8 to 9 p. m				2	2	6
9 to 10 p. m	1	1	1	2	5	8
10 to 11 p. m			2	2	1	7
11 to 12 p. m				1		1
	8	10	36	61	63	178

RELATION OF DISTRIBUTION OF SHOCKS TO DIURNAL VARIATIONS OF BAROMETRIC PRESSURE.

The grouping of the shocks suggests at once a relationship to barometric pressure, each of the periods of activities coinciding approximately with a barometric maximum or minimum. Assuming the maximums to occur at 10 a. m. and 9 p. m. and the minimums to occur at 3 a. m. and 4 p. m., and arranging the day into periods of two to five hours according to the intervals between the diurnal crests and troughs, it is found that the relation of shocks to barometer is very striking. This is well brought out in the following table:

Distribution of shocks with reference to barometric pressure.

Hour.	Barometer.	Violent shocks.	Severe shocks.	Moderate shocks.	Total.
12 to 5 a. m.	Minimum	3	2	11	16
5 to 8 a. m.	Intermediate		1	2	2
8 to 12 a. m.	Maximum	3	2	10	15
12 to 2 p. m.	Intermediate			4	4
2 to 5 p. m.	Minimum	1	2	5	8
5 to 7 p. m.	Intermediate		2	2	4
7 to 10 p. m.	Maximum		2	2	4
10 to 12 p. m.	Intermediate	1	1	2	4

The writer does not wish especially to support a relation between shocks and barometric maximums and minimums, but the figures of the table are so striking as to suggest that the relation is more than accidental. The use of the three higher shock intensities only is owing to the incomplete records for the lighter shocks, due to the absence of recording seismographs and the fact that the vibrations were too slight to awaken the people.

RELATION OF DISTRIBUTION OF SHOCKS TO PHASES OF THE MOON.

The attraction exerted by the sun and moon on the earth's surface at times of new and full moon is decidedly greater than during the intermediate periods and has been thought to be an appreciable factor in determining the times of earthquakes. In order to detect the relation that exists, if any, in the case of the New Madrid series of shocks, the writer obtained from Prof. Walter S. Harshman, Director of the Nautical Almanac Office, the dates of the moon's phases for 1811–12. These are as follows in Greenwich mean time:

	New moon.	Full moon.
	h. m.	*h. m.*
1811	Dec. 15........ 7 6	Dec. 29........ 7 31
1812	Jan. 13........ 20 27	Jan. 27........ 23 51
	Feb. 12........ 8 15	Feb. 26........ 18 4
	Mar. 12........ 18 32	Mar. 27........ 12 21
	Apr. 11........ 3 28	Apr. 26........ 5 8
	May 10........ 11 35	May 25........ 19 31

Figure 5 shows a curve representing the relative attractions of sun and moon at times of full and new moons and in intermediate periods (not to scale). On this is shown by symbols the distribution of the three most severe classes of shock, including (1) violent or "tremendous," (2) strong or severe, and (3) moderate or considerable. In general the shocks occur in groups beginning with violent and grading off into severe and moderate, although there are frequently two or more shocks of great severity. It is as if the first was the primary shock due to the formation of a fissure along which occur the minor movements reestablishing the equilibrium disturbed by the main shock and giving rise to the lesser shocks. With one marked exception the groups occur approximately either at times of new or full moon. There appears to be little difference in the activity at the two maximum periods.

With the minor shocks the conditions are somewhat different. In frequency these vary inversely with the number of severe shocks. In the first week, when several violent disturbances occurred, only 87 minor shocks are recorded. During the week ending June 26, which was marked by violent shocks, there were 91 minor disturbances, while during the week of February 9, also marked by tremendous shocks, the minor vibrations were less than in many intermediate periods. In fact, the records suggest that if the movements are considerable, as were those giving rise to the principal shocks, new equilibriums are established quickly, whereas a large number of minor movements are required to produce the same result. This explains why the minor shocks were fewest in the first quarter of the moon and the violent shocks were most numerous. The general relation of the number of shocks to the phases of the moon is indicated in the following table, based on the records of Brooks:[1]

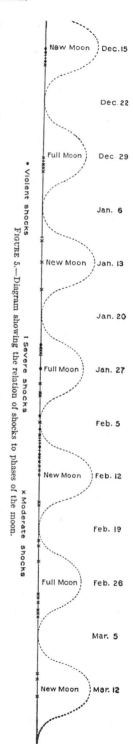

• Violent shocks   l Severe shocks   x Moderate shocks

FIGURE 5.—Diagram showing the relation of shocks to phases of the moon.

New Moon	Dec.15
	Dec.22
Full Moon	Dec. 29
	Jan. 6
New Moon	Jan. 13
	Jan. 20
Full Moon	Jan. 27
	Feb. 5
New Moon	Feb. 12
	Feb. 19
Full Moon	Feb. 26
	Mar. 5
New Moon	Mar. 12

---

[1] Brooks, Jared, op. cit., appendix.

Distribution of shocks with reference to phases of the moon.

[Based on table of Jared Brooks, reprinted on page 34.]

| Week ending. | Phase of moon. | | | Total shocks. |
	Phase.	Date.	General phase for week.	
1811.				
Dec. 22	New	Dec. 15	First quarter	87
Dec. 29	Full	Dec. 29	Second quarter	156
1812.			Third quarter	134
Jan. 5			Fourth quarter	161
Jan. 12	New	Jan. 13	First quarter	65
Jan. 19			Second quarter	91
Jan. 26	Full	Jan. 27	Third quarter	209
Feb. 2			Fourth quarter	175
Feb. 9	New	Feb. 12	First quarter	86
Feb. 16			Second quarter	292
Feb. 23	Full	Feb. 26	Third quarter	139
Mar. 1				58
Mar. 8	New	Mar. 12	Fourth quarter	221
Mar. 15				

Summary for quarters.

	First quarter.	Second quarter.	Third quarter.	Fourth quarter.
December–January	87	156	134	161
January–February	65	91	209	175
February–March	86	292	197	221
	238	539	540	557

RELATION OF THE EARTHQUAKE AND THE WEATHER.

There has been for some time a growing tendency to regard speculations as to the relations of earthquakes and weather as futile. So far as this applies to temperature and precipitation the tendency is probably warranted, but there appears to be reason to believe that the variations of pressure associated with cyclonic or storm movements are of more importance than is sometimes imagined. Variations of an inch in the length of the mercury column, which are by no means excessive, mean a change in pressure of half a pound per square inch, or 3⅓ per cent of the total atmospheric pressure. Such changes in pressure, especially when they are sudden, have profound effects. The water in deep wells often fluctuates materially with changes of barometric pressure; many wells flow during the passage of cyclonic centers which at other times fail to reach the surface; broad tidelike waves (seiches) several feet in height are not infrequently formed in the Great Lakes; and recent observations by Omori [1] near Tokyo, Japan, show that the passage of cyclonic storms sometimes even produces measurable tiltings of the earth's surface, the ground rising and falling as the cyclones progress.

[1] Nature, Sept. 26, 1907, p. 553; Science, new ser., vol. 26, p. 761.

No record of barometric pressures in the vicinity of New Madrid at the time of the earthquake seems to be available, but in view of the possible importance of the relation of earthquakes to variations of atmospheric pressure, it is pertinent to present the inferential evidence afforded by the general weather conditions in adjacent regions.

Very complete notes on the general weather conditions at Louisville were made by Jared Brooks.[1] These are abbreviated in the table on pages 22 to 26. From these it appears that the weather, although marked by long cloudy or stormy periods, was really not abnormal unless somewhat warmer than usual. In the time for which the record was kept, extending from December 16 to May 5, there were 100 fair, 42 cloudy, and 33 stormy days. A study of the shocks separately recorded shows that 89, or 0.89 per day, took place in pleasant weather, 100, or 2.38 per day, in cloudy weather, and 66, or 2 per day, during storms. The cloudy and the rainy weather should, however, be combined in a single class, since rain is a mere and uncertain incident to the cloudiness. This grouping gives 89 shocks, or 0.89 per day, in fair weather, as against 166, or 2.21 per day, in cloudy or stormy weather. The details of the shocks, as brought out more fully in the following table, seem to indicate that about twice as many shocks occurred in periods of low barometer (as indicated by cloudiness and rain) as in periods of high barometer, while the average number per day was nearly two and one-half times as great in stormy and unsettled weather as in fair weather.

Relation of shocks to the weather, as observed at Louisville, Ky.

[Based on table, pages 22 to 26.a]

Intensity.	Fair (100 days).		Cloudy, etc. (42 days).		Stormy (33 days).	
	Number of shocks.	Number of shocks daily.	Number of shocks.	Number of shocks daily.	Number of shocks.	Number of shocks daily.
Intense, violent	2	0.02	2	0.05	4	0.12
Strong, severe	5	.05	1	.02	4	.12
Moderate, considerable	13	.13	16	.38	15	.45
Strong vibrations, considerable vibrations, slight shocks	23	.23	21	.50	13	.40
Faint shocks, tremors, weak vibrations	46	.46	60	1.43	30	.90
	89	.89	100	2.38	66	2.00

a The lack of agreement as to the total numbers of the less severe shocks between this and the summary table of Brooks (p. 34) is due to the indefiniteness of some of the descriptions in Brooks's list.

DIRECTION OF VIBRATIONS.

The reports of the direction of vibrations are much less complete than could be wished, and of those available only a few represent instrumental determination, and even these were recorded on more or

---

[1] McMurtrie, H., Sketches of Louisville and its environs, Louisville, 1819, Appendix.

less imperfect home-made instruments. The recorded directions of the principal shocks are presented in the following table. The directions are also shown graphically in figure 1. The apparent directions of sounds are omitted as being too unreliable for record. The sounds appear to be produced by elastic waves of the same origin as the more powerful waves giving rise to the earth tremors and seem to be transmitted through the ground and communicated to the air just before they reach the ear. The general directions of the air vibrations would thus be upward and downward, giving rise to very illusory impressions.

It is interesting to note that vibrations capable of producing sound reached as far as Washington, D. C., and Charleston, S. C.

Directions from which vibrations of the New Madrid earthquake were reported as coming.

Locality.	Authority.	Dec. 16, 1811.	Dec. 17, 1811.	Jan. 23, 1812.	Feb. 7, 1812.	Feb. 8, 1812.	Feb. 17, 1812.	Feb. 22, 1812.
New Madrid, Mo...	Various...	SW.						
Herculaneum, Mo..	Mitchill...	SE.						
Columbia, Tenn....	...do.......	SW.						
Carthage, Tenn....	...do.......	SW.						
Louisville, Ky.....	Brooks....	{ SW.[1,2] S.[1,3] Vert.[1,4] }						
Cincinnati, Ohio...	Drake.....	W.		SSE.[1]	{ SW.[1] SSW.[1] SSE.[1] }	Vert.[1]	SSE.[1]	S.[1]
Lebanon, Ohio.....	Mitchill...	E.						
Detroit, Mich......	...do.......		SW.			Vert.[1]		
Charleston, S. C....	...do.......	S.(?)						
Savannah, Ga......	...do.......		SW.					
Washington, D. C..	...do.......	SW.						

[1] Instrumental determinations.   [2] Most.   [3] Few.   [4] Occasional.

From the table it appears that the direction of the vibrations at New Madrid was from the west, while at Herculaneum, which is northwest of New Madrid, the movement was from the southeast. At Red Bank and Cincinnati, northeast of New Madrid, the vibrations were from the west; but at Lebanon, not far from Cincinnati, they are reported to have been from the east. At Carthage and Columbia, Tenn., nearly due east of the area of greatest disturbance, the direction of the vibrations was from the southwest. At Washington, D. C., the movement was reported as northeastward.

Considering the difficulty in determining the direction from which a shock comes, even when the trend of the oscillation is known, it is perhaps surprising in the absence of any recording instruments that the records agree as well as they do. An example of this was presented in Lebanon, Ohio, where the movement was in an east-west direction, but whether propagated from the east or from the west could not be readily determined. It was reported as coming from the east, though it came, in all probability, from the west. In fact, except that from Lebanon, the observations on the direction of the first shock are all reasonably accordant, the slight variation shown at the Ohio River towns doubtless being due to local influence.

The direction of the shock of December 17 was recorded only at Detroit and Savannah, although it was felt at other places. The direction of the vibrations at the former city were normal for a shock originating in the New Madrid area, but at the latter city were somewhat abnormal, possibly owing to a local tendency to move in the line of least resistance toward the adjacent river.

The shock of January 23 was recorded by instruments at Cincinnati as from the south-southeast, which must be regarded as abnormal if the shock originated in the New Madrid area, but would be normal for a readjustment taking place in the Appalachians. It should be noted, however, that the shock was comparable in severity to that of December 16 in the New Madrid area, indicating that the focus could not have been very remote.

The shocks of February 7, often known as the big shocks, were three in number and were recorded in Charleston as from the southwest, south-southwest, and south-southeast. The two former are normal for a shock originating in the New Madrid area.

The shock of February 8 is notable for the apparently vertical character of its vibrations, which are reported from points as remote as Cincinnati and Detroit. No record of a shock on this date at New Madrid has been found, although very likely there was one. The same is true of the shocks of February 17 and 22.

EFFECT OF THE EARTHQUAKE ON LIFE.

As would be supposed from the severity of the disturbance, human beings nearly everywhere were terrified by the earlier shocks, their behavior giving rise to many ludicrous and many pathetic incidents. Even the lower animals shared the feelings of great alarm. The most graphic accounts of the feelings and behavior of the inhabitants during the shock are given by Drake, Mitchill, Foster, Bryan, LeSieur, Audubon, Wetmore, Carr, Bradbury, Brooks, and Cassedy. The effects on lower animals are described by Audubon, Bryan, Mitchill, Bradbury, Hildreth, and Flint. (See Bibliography, pp. 111 to 115.) Later, as the inhabitants became more familiar with the shocks, they lost much of the fear and began to observe the phenomena more closely. In Louisville and elsewhere swinging and spring pendulums were set up for the purpose of detecting the minor tremors and of distinguishing the horizontal and vertical movements. Jared Brooks, especially, conducted a long series of experiments, using pendulums from 1 to 6 inches in length, the results of which were recorded fully. (For summary, see pp. 22 to 26.)

The New Madrid earthquake caused very slight loss of life, as compared with most other earthquakes of similar intensity. Thus, at Caracas, which was destroyed during the continuance of the New Madrid shocks, over 10,000 were killed by falling walls, whereas in

the New Madrid area only a single life has been reported as lost in this manner. This immunity was due to the fact that the region of greatest disturbance was thinly settled and without large towns with brick or stone buildings to collapse and crush the inhabitants. In this country region the buildings were mainly cabins, which were strongly built and at the same time more or less elastic. The frame houses of the larger villages were likewise of a character to give before rather than resist the vibrations. The fact that the people left their houses at the first shock and were in places of comparative safety when the later and more severe shocks came also has much to do with their escape. The only death on land of which accounts have been seen was that of one woman who, frightened by the shock, ran until her strength gave out and expired of fear and exhaustion.[1] One writer tells of others who were thrown into the river by caving banks at New Madrid and drowned.[2] None of the contemporaneous accounts, however, seem to mention the latter incident. An account of a loss of life by the caving and disappearance of Island No. 94, near Vicksburg, is given by Broadhead.[3] Quoting from an old account of the trip of Capt. Sarpy, of St. Louis, he says:

They tied up at this island on the evening of the 15th of December, 1811. In looking around they found that a party of river pirates occupied part of the island and were expecting Sarpy with the intention of robbing him. As soon as Sarpy found that out he quietly dropped lower down the river. In the night the earthquake came and next morning when the accompanying haziness disappeared the island could no longer be seen. It had been utterly destroyed as well as its pirate inhabitants.

On the river a number were drowned. Bradbury mentions seeing drifting canoes, the owners of which he afterward found had been lost.[4] Hildreth describes the loss of several boats and their crews by caving banks.[5] Lloyd[2] records that a flat boat belonging to Richard Stump was swamped and six men drowned. Many other boats were destroyed by snags and the river was covered with wrecks. So numerous were the disasters that the escape and arrival at Natchez of Capt. Roosevelt with the steamer *New Orleans* was regarded as almost miraculous.

GOVERNMENT RELIEF.

The earthquake, as has been indicated, left many persons homeless, while the habitations of others were rendered so dangerous that the owners were compelled to take up their abode in tents or temporary huts for safety. Many farms were in whole or in part

[1] Flint, Timothy, Recollections of the last 10 years, Boston, 1826, pp. 222–228.
[2] Lloyd, J. T., Lloyd's steamboat directory, Cincinnati, 1856, p. 325.
[3] Broadhead, G. C., The New Madrid earthquake: Am. Geologist, vol. 30, 1902.
[4] Bradbury, John, Early western travels, Cleveland, 1904, vol. 5, p. 206.
[5] Hildreth, S. P., Original contributions to the American Pioneer, Cincinnati, 1844, pp. 34-35.

precipitated into the streams; others were covered by extruded waters; still others were depressed and gradually covered by accumulating surface waters. The aggregate loss of tillable land reached thousands of acres. Moreover, the continuance of the shocks gave rise to an uneasiness for the future which seriously retarded the recovery.

The loss and suffering were eventually brought to the attention of Congress, but in the light of subsequent events it is not certain to what extent assistance was the real object of the agitation or to what extent it was a pretext for land grabbing on the part of certain unscrupulous persons.

The agitation in Congress resulted in the passage of an act allowing those whose lands had been destroyed by the earthquake to locate the same quantity of land in any other part of the public domain open to entry. Few of the losers took advantage of this, however, for by this time the shocks had nearly ceased, the people had become adjusted to the new conditions and the prospects for the future looked fairly bright, even on the original lands. On this account the inhabitants were loath to go to the expense and hardships of removal to distant lands, but sold out their claims to new lands for whatever they would bring, usually only a few cents per acre. Five hundred and sixteen certificates were issued, but only 20 were located by the original claimants in person; most of the remainder were acquired by speculators in St. Louis. Perjury and forgery became so common that for a time a New Madrid claim was regarded as a synonym for fraud.[1]

PHENOMENA OF THE EARTHQUAKE.

ATMOSPHERIC PHENOMENA.

Darkness.—As in most of the great earthquakes the atmosphere seems to have become darkened during the more severe shocks in the Mississippi Valley. Eliza Bryan notes that total darkness accompanied the first shock, while a similar "awful darkness of the atmosphere" marked the severe shock of 4 p. m. on February 7.[2] Godfrey Le Sieur also says a "dense black cloud of vapor overshadowed the land" after the severe shocks.[2] At Herculaneum the atmosphere, according to Col. Samuel Hammond, was filled with smoke or fog so that a boat could not be seen 20 paces, and houses were so shrouded as not to be visible 50 feet. The air did not clear until the middle of the day.[3] A writer from New Madrid states that at the time of the shock the air was clear, but in five minutes it became very dark, and the darkness continued until nearly morning, during which period there were six shocks. At 6.30 the air cleared, but at the severe shock later in the morning the darkness returned.[4]

[1] Carr, Lucien, American Commonwealths: Missouri, Boston, 1888, p. 111.
[2] See Bibliography, pages 111–115.
[3] Mitchill, S. L., Trans. Lit. and Philos. Soc. New York, vol. 1, p. 291.
[4] Mitchill, S. L., op. cit., p. 297.

The darkness was probably due to a number of cooperating causes. In all probability the dust projected into the air by the agitation of the surface, the opening and closing of fissures in dry earth, landslides on dry hillsides, and possibly the falling of chimneys and buildings contributed to supply to the atmosphere the suspended particles which presumably produced the obscurity described. It is likely also that aqueous vapors, rising from fissures connecting with the warm ground waters (temperature 50° to 55°), or from the waters extruded from cracks and craterlets and condensed by the cold December air played a part. The extrusion of such vapors, usually more or less sulphurous, is described by many witnesses. It is not entirely impossible that conditions favoring condensation of atmospheric moisture either accompanied or resulted from the earthquake disturbance.

Besides the darkness observed in the area of principal disturbance similar manifestations were recorded in other localities. For instance, at Columbia, Tenn., a very large volume of something like smoke was declared to have risen in the southwest, from which direction the sound appeared to have come, and, proceeding northeastward, settled as a black cloud in the course of the 10 or 15 minutes the shock lasted.[1]

An unusual darkness during the earthquake was reported at a number of other points, but if it had any relation to the earth disturbances its nature is not known. It seems likely that in the outlying districts the darkness was due to ordinary clouds associated with storms then in progress across the country.

Odors and vapors.—Sulphurous or otherwise obnoxious odors and vapors were an attendant feature of the earthquake at many points, as stated by nearly every writer. Bryan speaks of the complete saturation of the atmosphere with sulphurous vapor a few minutes after the first shock, and of similar vapors after the shock of February 7.[2] Hildreth speaks of the escape of sulphur gas through the cracks tainting the air and impregnating the water for a distance of 150 miles so it was unfit to use.[2] Another observer, writing to Mitchill from New Madrid, states that although the air was clear at the time of the shock, within five minutes a vapor with a disagreeable smell and producing a difficulty of breathing impregnated the atmosphere. At Jeffersonville, Ind., warmth and smokiness were noted for several days after the shock, while at Columbia, S. C., the air during the shock felt impregnated with vapor which lasted for some time.

The source of the odors in the New Madrid region seems to have been the buried organic matter which here, as elsewhere in the Mississippi embayment, occurs in the alluvium and underlying Tertiary deposits, the emanations coming mainly from the carbonaceous

1 Mitchill, S. L., op. cit., p. 287.
2 See Bibliography, pages 111-115.

material extruded from below through the fissures and craterlets, which were numerous in the region. In the more remote localities the vapors probably represented normal atmospheric condensations which happened to be coincident with the earthquake disturbance.

"Light flashes" and "glows."—The phenomena of what may be termed "light flashes" and "glows" seem so improbable that they would be dismissed from consideration but for the considerable number of localities from which they were reported. Dillard, in speaking of the shocks (not especially the first one), says: "There issued no burning flames, but flashes such as would result from an explosion of gas, or from passing of electricity from cloud to cloud." Lewis F. Linn, United States Senator, in a letter to the chairman of the Committee on Commerce, says the shock was accompanied "ever and anon [by] flashes of electricity, rendering the darkness doubly terrible." [1] Another evidently somewhat excited observer near New Madrid thought he saw "many sparks of fire emitted from the earth." [2] At St. Louis gleams and flashes of light were frequently visible around the horizon in different directions, generally ascending from the earth.[3] In Livingston County, according to Mr. Riddick, the atmosphere previous to the shock of February 8 was remarkably luminous, objects being visible for considerable distances, although there was no moon. "On this occasion the brightness was general, and did not proceed from any point or spot in the heavens. It was broad and expanded, reaching from the zenith on every side toward the horizon. It exhibited no flashes nor coruscations, but, as long as it lasted, was a diffused illumination of the atmosphere on all sides." At Bardstown there are reported to have been "frequent lights during the commotions." [4] At Knoxville, Tenn., at the end of the first shock, "two flashes of light, at intervals of about a minute, very much like distant lightning," were observed.[5] Farther east, in North Carolina, there were reported "three large extraordinary fires in the air; one appeared in an easterly direction, one in the north, and one in the south. Their continuance was several hours; their size as large as a house on fire; the motion of the blaze was quite visible, but no sparks appeared." [6] At Savannah, Ga., the first shock is said to have been preceded by a flash of light.[7]

That the flashes were entirely imaginary is improbable, but it is very doubtful if anything out of the ordinary actually took place. A source of many of the flashes appears to have been the thunder storms which occurred at the time. Such storms, which were very unusual at the season at which the shocks took place and which were

---

[1] Wetmore, Alphonso, Gazetteer of the State of Missouri, St. Louis, 1837, pp. 131-142.
[2] Mitchill, S. L., Trans. Lit. and Philos. Soc. New York, vol. 1, p. 300.
[3] Idem, p. 288.
[4] Idem, p. 298.
[5] Idem, p. 287.
[6] Idem, p. 300.
[7] Idem, p. 286.

unsuspected by the people outside of their immediate path, have been recorded at a number of points, especially in South Carolina.[1] Bearing on the origin of the flashes or glows the observations of several of the captains of ocean liners in the Tropics at the time of the recent severe disturbance in Mexico (1907) are of significance. They reported that on the night on which they afterwards learned that the earthquake had occurred strong glows in the sky, resembling the auroras of northern latitudes, were seen. As these were not reported farther north the view suggests itself that they were due to magnetic disturbances depending upon or related to the severe earth disturbances going on at the time. It is not improbable that similar magnetic manifestations were associated with the New Madrid shock.

It is probable that in the New Madrid region brush or wood fires, made by the Indians or settlers, may have been an additional cause. It should be noted in this connection that in the New Madrid area itself, where the weather was clear at the time, no mention of any such phenomena was made in the more conservative descriptions.

GEOLOGIC PHENOMENA.

FISSURES.

RECORD OF FISSURING.

Fissuring was one of the most common and widespread of the phenomena resulting from the New Madrid earthquake and is mentioned in practically all contemporaneous narratives. Among the most vivid accounts is that of Le Sieur, who says [2] that the earth rolled in waves several feet high with visible depressions between the swells, finally bursting and leaving parallel fissures extending in a north-south direction for distances as great as 5 miles in some cases. Dillard [3] describes the opening of fissures 600 to 700 feet long and 20 to 30 feet wide. Some were sufficiently wide to swallow horses or cattle [4] and in one instance a load of castings disappeared from a cellar.[5] Another type, of smaller size but of even more general distribution, was that resulting from the settling and caving of the river banks, as described by Bradbury.[6] Again, Hildreth says "the earth on the shores opened in wide fissures," and Flint states that some persons were extricated from them with difficulty,[7] while Flint and others describe the felling of trees crosswise with the trend of the fissuring, on which persons climbed as a protection against engulfment. Latrobe, in relating the experience of a boatman, says [8] that

[1] Mitchill, S. L., op. cit., pp. 285–286.
[2] Le Sieur, Godfrey, quoted in Am. Geologist, vol. 30, 1902, p. 80.
[3] Foster, J. W., The Mississippi Valley, Chicago, 1869, pp. 19–22.
[4] Flint, Timothy, Recollections of the last ten years, Boston, 1826, p. 226.
[5] Hildreth, S. P., Original contributions to the American Pioneer, Cincinnati, 1844, pp. 34–35.
[6] Bradbury, John, Early western travels, Cleveland, 1904, vol. 5, p. 205.
[7] Flint, Timothy, op. cit., p. 223.
[8] Latrobe, C. J., The rambler in North America, London, 1836, vol. 1, pp. 107–108.

a chasm opened in the Mississippi admitting great quantities of water, but immediately closed, giving rise to waves of great size. From many of the fissures it was stated that sand and water were forcibly extruded.

CHARACTER OF THE FISSURES.

Fortunately it is not necessary to rely on the contemporary accounts of the fissuring, as many of the cracks are still well preserved, and the position of others is marked by extruded materials, or occasionally by sand dikes filling the original fissures.

Types.—There are two distinct types of what are here spoken of as fissures. The first is the simple crack, which is either open at the present time or is filled with sand extruded when formed or by débris which has fallen in subsequently. The second type, although for convenience spoken of as a fissure because of its considerable depth, appears to be in reality a narrow down-faulted block between two parallel cracks, as indicated in figure 6. The sharp depressions, often many feet in depth and width and of great length, seem to be all of this type. Plate II, *A*, shows one side of such a fissure, the drop

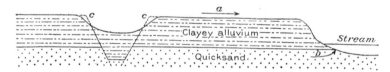

FIGURE 6.—Diagram showing trench or "fissure" formed by settling of fault block. *a*, Direction of movement of upper alluvium toward stream; *b*, Direction of flowage of quicksand; *c*, Original walls of trench before slump.

of the central segment being about 4 feet and its width (not shown) about 15 feet. In most of the simple fissures there has been no vertical movement of the walls, but occasionally low faults are seen. No extrusion of sand has been noted from the fault block or the simple faulted fissures.

Form.—The form varies considerably with the location and type of fissures. The simple cracks are on the whole much more irregular than the compound fissures. They are seldom straight for any great distance. Those near the margins of the rivers often partake of the curvature of the banks. Those across points of land in oxbows of the river are commonly irregular and branching. Those of the flat bottoms in sand-blow districts appear to be in most cases short, interrupted, and more or less crooked fissures, although a few are straight. The larger fault-block fissures are often straight for considerable distances, although usually exhibiting more or less irregularity of direction throughout their course. Lyell,[1] in describing such fissures near New Madrid, says: "Some of them were jagged, others even and straight * * *. I might easily have mistaken them

---

[1] Lyell, Charles, A second visit to the United States, London, 1849, p. 235.

for artificial trenches." This characteristic, in fact, is very general in this type of fractures, especially in those in the area southwest of Lake St. Francis, where the sharp steep sides and flat bottoms are especially suggestive of canal excavations.

Arrangement.—The arrangement depends upon the type and situation. The simple fissures along river banks are usually in concentric curves. Where the deposits tended more to disintegration during the shock, as on long points of land, a complex of jagged branching fissures commonly resulted. In the flat lands of the sand-blow country there appears to be a general tendency to an arrangement in parallel lines, but owing to the shortness of many of the gashes this is not always apparent. In the large fault-block fissures the parallelism is generally very marked, groups of from two to five or more long, straight, and parallel canal-like depressions being not uncommon.

Intervals.—The spacing of the fissures is very variable. They are closest together when near the banks of rivers, parallel cracks only a foot or two apart sometimes occurring, while a spacing of from 10 to 15 feet is not uncommon. In the sand-blow districts the spacing varies from several hundred feet down to less than 10 feet, the resulting extrusions in the latter case forming more or less confluent sheets of sand. The spacing in the caving ground on points is still less. In the case of the large fault-block fissures the spacing is greater, several hundred feet often intervening between the cracks, while the space between them may be half a mile or more. Isolated cracks of this type are not uncommon.

Direction.—The direction of the fissures is of much interest because of the light it might be expected to throw upon the question of the center of disturbance and the direction of the earth waves. In considering the direction, however, three classes of fissures must be differentiated. The first, or the simple cracks near streams, are, as already indicated, almost invariably parallel with the banks of the rivers, occurring in any and all directions, but apparently entirely independent of the direction of the earthquake waves. The second class, or the simple fissures of the sand-blow areas seem to have a tendency toward a definite arrangement along northeast-southwest lines (averaging about N. 30° E.), although where the blows are scattered the arrangement is not always very apparent. The fissures of the sand sloughs are in general parallel to the depressions and are even more commonly aligned in northeast-southwest directions.

In the third class, or the compound or fault-block fissures, the tendency is not always so manifest. In the area southwest of Lake St. Francis (T. 9 N., R. 5 E.), which was studied in most detail, the majority of the cracks have a trend very close to the bearing mentioned, being apparently independent of the course of the river

near which they are located (fig. 7).   There are, however, at least
two compound fissures nearly at right angles to the others.

Of those who observed the fissures soon after their formation,
Flint has given the most specific statement of their direction, which
he states was generally from northeast to southwest. Lyell in describing those near New Madrid says:[1] "They varied greatly in direction,
some being 10° and others 45° west of north."

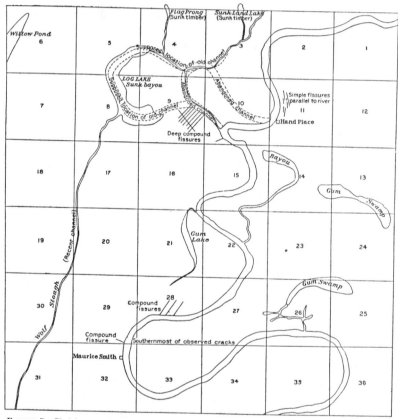

FIGURE 7.—Sketch map showing earthquake features southwest of Lake St. Francis. The lines
indicating fissures are intended to show location and general direction but not the specific number of the fractures.

It is a question if the statement credited to Lyell is not a misprint,
as most other observers have recorded them as east of north. In
fact, except in the case of the local fissures manifestly due to the
creep or disintegration of the river banks and points, practically
all the evidence supports the existence of a northeast-southwest
trend of the fissuring of both simple and compound types throughout
the entire area examined.

[1] Lyell, Charles, A second visit to the United States, London, 1849, p. 235.

Length.—The length of the fissures varies considerably. Some of the narrow ones of the simple type appear to be only a few yards long, but others may be 100 to 200 feet or even more in length. Probably 300 feet is the maximum for this type, both when occurring along the river banks or in the broad flat sand-blow districts. The length of the compound or fault-block fissures, however, is much greater. Those along the St. Francis River north of Parkin are said to be half a mile or so long (fig. 7), while others doubtless have even greater length, as the fissures cited by Le Sieur, which he reported to have a length of 5 miles. The average length for cracks of this type is estimated to be from 300 to 500 feet. East of the Mississippi the fissuring was in general less pronounced, but Usher[1] mentions cracks of some size extruding for miles.

Depth.—The depth of the openings was not usually very great, probably being in most cases limited to the hard clayey zone extending from the surface down to the quicksand which usually underlies the surface soil at depths of from 10 to 20 feet (fig. 6). Few openings probably extended much below the water level, which is apparently nowhere much over 25 feet from the surface. The fissures locally extended somewhat deeper but did not long remain open, owing to the presence of water and quicksand. Flint[2] speaks of the fissures as "fearfully deep" at the time of his visit seven years after the shock, although formed in soft alluvium. Lyell, speaking of the trenchlike cracks near New Madrid, says[3] that his informant stated that within his recollection these were "as deep as wells." At the time of his visit they were only 5 or 6 feet deep, although, as he says: "The action of rains, frost, and occasional inundations, and above all, the leaves of the forest blown into them every autumn in countless numbers, have done much to fill them up."

The deepest fissures seen by the writer, outside the landslide area of the Chickasaw Bluffs, were in the St. Francis River region south of the lake. Several of the compound fissures here were so deep that when riding on horseback in their bottoms his head was below the level of the surrounding flats. Plate II, *A*, shows one side of one of the smaller of these fissures, the scarp being about 4 feet high. Several rather deep cracks were also seen at Marked Tree.

The present depth of the simple fissures was nowhere found to be more than a foot or two, owing to their becoming filled by the caving of the sides. Of the smaller fissures, such as those of the sand-blow area, no surface indications remain other than the extruded material.

Fillings (sand dikes).—The filling of the fissures by the caving of the walls has already been mentioned. Besides this, however, should be mentioned the fillings of intruded materials from below.

1 Usher, F. C., Am. Jour. Sci., 1st ser., vol. 31, 1837, p. 295.
2 Flint, Timothy, Recollections of the last 10 years, Boston, 1826, p. 223.
3 Lyell, Charles, A second visit to the United States, London, 1847, p. 235.

As described elsewhere (pp. 76 to 87), the formation of fissures was almost always accompanied by the extrusion of sand and water which flowed out over the surrounding surface. Besides the fissures which reached the surface, many pinched out before the top of the ground was reached, and the sand had no opportunity to escape but remained in the crack as a sand dike after the cessation of the shock. Even where the fissures reached the surface more or less sand was caught in the cracks and was left as stringers and dikes in the darker alluvium. (See Pl. III.) Probably the sand-blow region is full of such dikes, but owing to the fact that few cellars or other excavations are made, because of the frequent overflow and dampness of the region, sections showing them are rare. They are, however, rather abundant at certain points on the higher ground, especially at Charleston and Campbell, Mo., and vicinity, several sometimes being exposed in a single excavation. That shown in Plate III is said to be one of several in the same cellar.

Objects swallowed by fissures.—Considering the number and frequency of fissures it at first seems surprising that so few objects were swallowed. It should be borne in mind, however, that the fissures were of two kinds, one due to the down-faulting of narrow strips of earth (fig. 6, p. 48), and the other to the cracking of the soil by tension as the earth waves progressed across the surface. The first made wide and deep depressions, which, however, had firm bottoms with nothing in the nature of deep chasms. The second were actual fissures. They were a few inches wide and extended to considerable depths, although probably rarely to the unfathomable depths which the people in their excitement were inclined to believe. The deepest one of which we have a measurement is 20 feet. The fear of being swallowed by the fissures led many to fell trees, at right angles to the direction of the fissures previously formed, upon which they climbed for safety at times of severe shocks when new fissures were to be expected. Many attributed their preservation to this practice. As a matter of fact, however, nothing except a boatload of castings, which had been stored in a cellar,[1] and a few tree trunks [2] appear to have been swallowed in the crevices, although a few persons extricated themselves from them with difficulty.

DISTRIBUTION OF THE FISSURES.

Situation.—The situation of the fissures has been indicated in the foregoing discussion, but may be summarized here. In general it may be said that the phenomena of fissuring may be seen on the uplands as well as the lowlands, but that in the former situation they are limited to the vicinity of the edges of steep bluffs and are not seen where the surface is flat or the slopes gentle, the absence of

---

[1] Foster, J. W., The Mississippi Valley, Chicago, 1869, pp. 19–22.
[2] Lloyd, James, Lloyd's steamboat directory, Cincinnati, 1856, p. 325.

EARTHQUAKE FISSURE FILLED WITH INTRUDED SAND, CHARLESTON. MO.

Photograph by Thomas Beckwith.

A. TREES TILTED BY NEW MADRID EARTHQUAKE, CHICKASAW BLUFFS, TENN.

B. CYPRESS TRUNKS KILLED BY SUBMERGENCE RESULTING FROM NEW MADRID EARTHQUAKE, LAKE ST. FRANCIS, ARK.

fissuring in such situations being due to the distance of the highland rims from the center of disturbance. Visible fissures are absent from most of the prairie ridges standing a few feet above the lowlands, because the superficial alluvial beds to which most of the fracturing was confined are there thicker than on the surrounding lowlands. In the northern part of the area the prairie deposits are more sandy and incoherent, and fissures, if they were formed at all, must have closed almost immediately.

The broad, flat alluvial bottoms of Mississippi, Little, and St. Francis rivers seem to have afforded very favorable conditions for the development of minor fissures, for the blows marking the extrusions from them are of wide distribution. The most favorable points, however, seem to be the broad linear depressions resulting from the sinking of the land. Here, if the extruded sand so characteristic of the sloughs is relied upon, the fissuring must have been even more common than on the surrounding flatlands. Fissuring in the bottoms of bayous was also very common, and in some instances is said to have led to the draining of the waters. (See p. 54.)

Localities.—The general distribution of fissuring can best be seen by reference to the maps (Pl. I and fig. 1). In the figure the areas of intense and moderate earthquake action are shown. Stream banks were caved northward to Herculaneum, northeastward to Indiana, southward to the Arkansas, and probably westward throughout the valleys of Black, Cache, and White rivers. The region showing fissuring is much smaller, being limited to the area extending from the vicinity of New Madrid to a point on the St. Francis a little northwest of Memphis. The most profound fissuring (compound type) observed by the writer was along the St. Francis and Tyronza rivers in the area delineated on Plate I and shown in detail in figure 10, but it is possible that similar fissuring extends farther north, although no marked examples were seen at Blytheville. The minor fissuring, giving rise to the sand blows, was mainly limited to the region between a point northwest of New Madrid and the lower end of Lake St. Francis, as shown on Plate I, but similar though less extensive fissuring also occurred east of the Mississippi from southwestern Kentucky southward at least as far as the mouth of the Obion River. Fissuring also occurs near the edge of the uplands, terminating in the Chickasaw Bluffs, from near Hickman on the Mississippi to beyond the Obion River. No marked fissuring of recent date was noted in Crowley Ridge, but faulted strata, due to early Pleistocene disturbances, were seen near Wittsburg, east of Wynne.

The most northerly cracks of which evidences were noted by the writer were in the woods along the Castor River northeast of Bloomfield, where there are several cracks parallel to the river (one of them cutting an Indian mound) and one at right angles to the stream. Cracks were also observed parallel to a cypress bayou near La Forge, north of New Madrid. At New Madrid, which is near the northern limits of the area of marked disturbance, fissures were originally common, but many have now been obliterated by the encroachments of the river, which has cut into the banks half a mile or more since the earthquake, by the overflowing waters, by the gradual accumulation of silts and vegetable muck, and by the cultivation of the land. Lyell, on his visit to the region in 1849, saw several fissures still open, two of which he traced continuously for over half a mile. Some were parallel, but most of them varied greatly in direction. In depth the simple fissures ranged up to 5 or 6 feet, and in width from 2 to 4 feet, the edges being marked by accumulations of sand and dark clayey shale. He also describes a fault produced by the earthquake which separated the higher level plain from the low ground about Bayou St. John just east of New Madrid. The descent was 8 or 10 feet at this point, although it was reported to be as much as 20 or 30 feet in places.[1] Two parallel fissures, about 8 yards apart, through which the waters of Lake Eulalie escaped after the earthquake, could still be seen in the bottom of the dry bed.

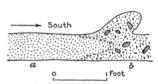

FIGURE 8.—Plan of earthquake fissure at Beechwell, near Campbell, Mo. a, Clayey alluvium; b, intruded sand and lignite.

Near Portageville, a few miles southwest of New Madrid, on Little River, large cracks were observed by the writer on both sides of the river, and smaller cracks occur in the vicinity of Marston, a short distance away. At Beechwell, just northeast of Campbell, a fine section of a fissure filled with sand, pieces of lignite, and dark shaly clay, was seen in a trench. This appears to have been pushed diagonally upward into the clayey alluvium, but not with sufficient force, at least on one side, to break through, the fissure terminating in a rounded head both in horizontal and vertical directions (fig. 8).

Many similar fissures are found in digging cellars in the vicinity of Charleston, some distance to the northeast (Pl. III), some failing to reach the surface, as in the instance described, while others reached the surface and formed sand blows.

At Caruthersville, as at New Madrid, fissures were originally very numerous, but many were obliterated by the overflowing waters of the Mississippi before the construction of the levees, and by the other causes mentioned. Traces of cracks are still to be seen near the creeks and bayous. Near Carlton, between Caruthersville and Hayti, a number of faults and gashes occur south of the railroad. Most of the scars at this point seem to have an east-west direction, but one or two north-south scars occur.

[1] Lyell, Charles, A second visit to the United States, pp. 235–236.

Farther southwest on the Pemiscot is the site of the smoke-house incident related by Le Sieur.[1] It seems that a Mr. Culberson lived on a V-shaped point in a bend of Pemiscot River, embracing about an acre of ground, on which his well and smokehouse were situated, lying between the house and the river. On the morning of the earthquake Mrs. Culberson started to go to the smokehouse for meat, only to find the path crossed by the wide stream, the smoke-house and well being seen across the river, on the opposite side from where they were the night before. Numerous cracks were made across such points, some of which afforded shorter courses to the streams. Near Blytheville, east of the Pemiscot, several cracks were observed along an old bayou.

Visible fissuring occurs at Lake City, on Lake St. Francis, and it is stated that crevices can be made out in the old river banks beneath the surface of the water. It is probable that other fissures, both numerous and large, would be found if the lakes and sunk lands were drained of their waters. At Marked Tree, south of Lake St. Francis, cracks 3 to 6 feet deep and 6 to 15 feet wide, extending for some dis-tance, are found on the east side of St. Francis River, and smaller, more irregular, and branching cracks occur on the west side. One of the cracks passes through the lumber yard at Marked Tree, cutting an Indian mound. This crack is now filled with standing water during wet seasons. Similar cracks occur along St. Francis and Little rivers for 12 miles, reaching into Mississippi County (Pl. I), while others are found along Tyronza River and south and southeast of Marked Tree. Cracks were seen at intervals below Marked Tree as far as the Maurice Smith place, in sec. 29, T. 9 N., R. 5 E., and are reported to occur near the bend of the river a mile farther to the southeast, this point being the southernmost limit of recorded fissur-ing. Figure 7 shows the distribution of the fissures in this region. The northernmost cracks in the township are north of the Hand place, in sec. 11. These are of the simple fissure type, from 10 to 100 or more feet long and 4 to 12 inches wide, and are concentric with the curve of the river bend at that point. A mile and a half farther west, in sec. 9, a series of northeast-southwest compound fissures of great size were observed. These are great canal-like depressions with flat bottoms and steep sides (higher even than the normal angle of repose) and so deep that a man on horseback is in some places unable to see over the top. It is probable that some of the depressions are from 10 to 15 feet deep, and the bottoms are usually from 10 to 20 feet in width. One large cross fracture mainly at right angles to the others was observed, and 3 miles south in sec. 28 three or four more large compound fissures were seen having a northeast-southwest

---

[1] Le Sieur, Godfrey, quoted in Am. Geologist, vol. 30, 1902, pp. 80-81.

trend. The Smith place fracture, already mentioned, was some 4 feet deep and 20 feet across at the bottom.

On the east side of the Mississippi the visible fissures, although less numerous than on the west side, were not uncommon. Usher [1] describes a fissure 4 feet deep and 8 feet wide, extending several miles. Lyell records several fissures in Tennessee where the ground on one side remained 2 feet higher than on the other. The writer is convinced that faulting of at least 10 feet occurred at places in the vicinity of the south end of Reelfoot Lake and it is known that fissures occur in the uplands at the edge of the Chickasaw Bluffs. David Dale Owen, in his report of the geological survey in Kentucky (1854-55) states on page 119 that "in Obion County, Tenn., depressions are even now visible 100 feet deep and varying from a few feet to upward of 100 feet wide, which are said to have been more than double this depth when originally formed." At another point "in the bluffs of the Mississippi earth cracks can be traced for a quarter to half a mile, 20 to 70 feet wide, bounded on either side by parallel banks 1 to 5 feet above the sunk ground." N. S. Shaler describes "earth cracks" as occurring at many points in the southwest corner of Kentucky, "the fissures being from 20 to 70 feet wide and 1 to 4 feet deep." [2] To these instances the writer can add small faults near Push and near Grace post office and a more conspicuous one parallel to Bluebank at the southern end of Reelfoot Lake. The sinking along the latter fault was about 6 feet.

Besides the fissuring giving rise to visible cracks those openings from which the materials of the sand blows and sand sloughs were extruded should be mentioned. The area in which these occur is indicated in the discussion of the blows and sloughs and its characteristics are considered in an earlier part of this section.

CAUSE OF FISSURING.

Bluff fissures.—In this class are included the simple fissures found near the edge of river bluffs, along the flanks of deep bayous, and near the edge of the uplands terminating in the Chickasaw Bluffs. These fissures have clearly been produced either by the actual settling of the land nearest the channel, valley, or other depression, the movement being away from the higher stationary ground, or by a partial undermining and tilting of the materials comprising the immediate banks of the streams. Where a material settling has occurred in addition to the lateral displacement, faults are produced. These fissures, as would be expected, merge into landslide disturbances. In fact, the explanation advanced appears to account satisfactorily for all the observed facts of occurrence and distribution.

[1] Usher, F. C., Am. Jour. Sci., 1st ser., vol. 31, 1837, p. 295.
[2] Shaler, N. S., Earthquakes of the western United States, Atlantic Monthly, November, 1869, p. 555.

Fissures of the sand-blow regions.—The fissures from which the materials of the sand blows and sloughs were extruded were probably produced as described in the contemporary narratives. It is known that, owing to the unusually favorable conditions existing (a thin surface stratum of stiff alluvium resting on a quicksand saturated with water as shown in fig. 6), earth waves of unusual magnitude, sometimes several feet in height, were propagated across the country, and there is every reason to suppose that numerous fissures resulted from this sudden flexing as they did at the time of the Charleston shock 75 years later. This "bursting of the swells," as it was termed by the eyewitnesses, is not only the possible but the probable cause of the fissuring, fully accounting for the distribution of the cracks, for their arrangement, and for their great numbers.

Fissuring of the sand sloughs.—The fissures of the sloughs appear to be longer than those associated with the sand blows, but do not seem to differ in other respects. It is believed that they are due to the same processes of flexure, the principal difference being that while the surface in the sand-blow areas became flat again after the passage of the waves, that of the sloughs remained bent, giving rise to the troughs in which they are now found.

Analogous to the slough fissures are the faults and cracks which sometimes separate the higher from the lower parts of the bottom lands. They are believed likewise to have resulted from warping, which, however, was on a much larger scale, the difference in level being so great and the change so sharp that fracture resulted.

Compound fissures.—The so-called compound fissures are believed to be the result of the dropping of a narrow fault block between two parallel simple fissures. The flatness of the bottom and the presence of trees antedating the shock seem to indicate that the present contour of the depression is due rather to the dropping of a block than to filling in from the sides of the fissure. There is an absence of gradation between the steep walls and the flat bottoms that would also be difficult to account for if a simple fissure had been partly filled by wash.

In order that the block between the parallel fissures should sink it is necessary that there should be either an outward movement of the material at one or both sides or an undermining of adequate extent. (See fig. 6, p. 48.) From examination it appears that such fissures are generally very near to rivers. The fissuring, however, is not always parallel to the stream, as would seem to be necessary if it was a lateral creep toward the river which permitted the sinking. In the majority of cracks of this type there was no extrusion of sand, hence the undermining can not be due to the transfer of material to the surface through fissures in the immediate vicinity. There remains the undermining by extrusion through more distant sand blows or undermining by creep of the quicksand into the rivers. From exposures in the bottom of the streams at low water it seems probable that the latter action took place to a considerable extent, and it is believed that in it lies the explanation of the sinking of the blocks of the great compound fissures.

FAULTS.

Location.—Faulting, at least in the surficial deposits, was not a common nor a characteristic feature of the New Madrid earthquake, although it occurred at a number of points. Some of the faults crossed the Mississippi, causing rapids and even waterfalls. William Shaler [1] in describing a patron's trip down the river at the time says that a few miles above New Madrid "he came to a most terrific fall, which, he thinks, was at least 6 feet perpendicular, extending across the river. * * * Another fall was formed about 8 miles below the town, similar to the one above, the roaring of which he could distinctly hear at New Madrid. He waited five days for the fall to wear away." Speaking of the fissures on the land in the vicinity of the town mentioned, he says many of them were "5 or 6 feet wide, extending in length out of sight, and one side was several feet lower than the other." Lyell [2] describes a fault, possibly the same as that noted by Shaler, separating the higher level plain from the low ground about Bayou St. John just east of town, the descent being 8 to 10 feet at this point. He also records several fissures in Tennessee where the ground on one side remained 2 feet higher than that on the other.

At the present time evidences of faults are hard to find, owing to the modification of the bottoms by the overflowing river. The writer, however, noted a scarp along a gently sloping hillside at Beechwell, near Campbell, Mo., the displacement of which seems to have been 10 feet or more. Small faults were also noted on the flat bottom lands near Push and Grace post offices in the vicinity of Reelfoot Lake, Tenn., and parallel to Bluebank at the southern end of Reelfoot Lake. The displacement at the latter point was about 6 feet. Still other faults are believed to have been formed about the south end of the lake mentioned, contributing to the damming of its waters.

Besides those mentioned there are a considerable number of faults parallel to a stream, where the land next the river has sunk below the landward side of the fissures. In the landslide areas much displacement has also taken place, as is described in the section on landslides (p. 59). Nearly all the principal fissures appear to have resulted from the dropping of narrow fault blocks, as described on pages 48 and 57.

[1] Shaler, William, Trans. Lit. and Philos. Soc. New York, vol. 1, p. 301.
[2] Lyell, Charles, A second visit to the United States, London, 1849, pp. 235-236.

Cause.—The faults appear to have resulted from various causes. Those formed across the Mississippi near New Madrid ponding the water back and giving rise to waterfalls almost certainly resulted from fractures incident to the uplift of the Tiptonville dome (p. 63). Those about the southern end of Reelfoot Lake appear to be due to the same general cause. The fault described by Lyell along the Bayou St. John apparently resulted from the settling of the land nearest the river, doubtless due to undermining resulting from the extrusion of the underlying quicksands or to their lateral flowage toward the river. At Beechwell there appears to have been a general movement of the lower hillside toward the flats, leaving a long high scarp. The faulting parallel to the river is unquestionably due to a displacement and slump toward the river, while the dropped fault blocks appear to have been let down by undermining, as explained on page 57.

LANDSLIDES.

Probably no feature of the earthquake is more striking than the landslides developed in certain of the steeper bluffs, even the casual observer noting at once the unusual character of the highly disturbed slopes. Landslides in the general sense of the term occurred whenever a slope had sufficient steepness so that portions gave way during the shock and slipped or fell down the grade toward the lower levels. The necessary conditions were presented by both the river banks and the higher bluffs bordering the Mississippi lowlands, especially on the east side. The breaking down of the river banks was very extensive, being observed, as noted on page 53, at least as far up the Ohio as Indiana and doubtless extending down the Mississippi a corresponding distance. The action in the case of the bluffs was more limited in area but often far greater in magnitude. The area characterized by minor disturbances, such as the caving of banks, is indicated in figure 1, and the principal landslide area is shown on Plate I.

CHICKASAW BLUFFS.

Location and character.—The area of landslides lies along the Chickasaw Bluffs, which face the Mississippi bottoms from the vicinity of Hickman in southwestern Kentucky at least to the mouth of the Obion River, about halfway across the State of Tennessee, a distance of at least 35 miles.

Throughout this distance the landslides are a striking feature. Skirting the edge of the bluffs, in the vicinity of Reelfoot Lake, a characteristic landslide topography is almost constantly in sight from the carriage road which follows their base, the road in some places crossing over large masses of earth brought down by the earthquake and winding among the trunks of the trees tilted by the movement. (See Pl. IV, *A*.) On climbing up the bluff the traveler sees increased confusion; sharp ridges of earth alternate with deep gashes (Pl. IV, *B*), the whole surface locally being broken into a jumble of irregular ridges, mounds, and hummocks, interspersed with trench or basinlike hollows and other more irregular depressions, continuing with increasing frequency to the top of the bluff, along the edge of which fault scarps and fissures are of frequent occurrence. Some of the depressions, those between parallel fissures, have the same canal-like aspect that characterizes those of the river bottoms (p. 48), but some are considerably larger, one reported by Safford [1] being as much as 100 feet wide. Speaking of Obion County, Tenn., Shaler says [2] "depressions are even now visible [1869] 100 feet deep and varying from a few feet to 100 feet wide."

Landslide fissures are best developed on projecting spurs, the main cracks crossing them in a direction at right angles to their axis. Where the surfaces had considerable curvature the slumping occurred in several directions, giving rise to intersecting fissures with mound-like elevations between.

Although landslides are most strongly developed on spurs, the general slopes of the bluffs are far from being free from them, and some of the resultant mounds and troughs are of considerable magnitude. One of these troughs, having a depth of between 6 and 8 feet, is shown in Plate II, *B*. Water has collected in some of them, forming small ponds. The individual troughs are generally of considerable length, often several hundred feet. They begin as very slight depressions in the surface of the bluff, which, however, rapidly widen and deepen until strong trenches are produced. The troughs are usually not exactly parallel to the slope; the bottom descends slightly as the trough widens, and it usually has free drainage at the low end or that farthest from its point of beginning. The individual troughs and ridges are more or less curved or irregular. Many of them begin and end abruptly; others divide and subdivide, only to reunite again, forming a network of trenches.

The movement in many cases has been such as to cause a tilting of the disturbed masses, the inclination being usually toward the bluff. The steep alluvial and débris fans at the mouths of the gullies extending back into the bluffs also seem to have afforded very favorable conditions for slumping, and many of them, even at the present time, exhibit corrugations and low fault scarps due to the flowage and slumping of the material toward the lowlands.

Not the least conspicuous feature of the slides is the tilting of the older trees which, at many points, stand sharply inclined to the surface just as they were placed by the earthquake, except for a gradual

---

[1] Safford, J. M., Geology of Tennessee, 1869, p. 113.

[2] Shaler, N. S., Earthquakes of the western United States: Atlantic Monthly, Nov., 1869, p. 555.

recovery of the perpendicular by the higher growth. This feature is described in detail on a subsequent page (p. 96), and is illustrated by Plate IV, *A*.

Among the localities in which landslides occurred the east side of Reelfoot Lake is the most interesting. Going south from Samburg to Push, the traveler has the landslides almost constantly in view. Some of the scars on the bluff are from 10 to 20 feet high and 200 feet long, and faults extending across the fans from the side ravines may often be seen. One and one-half miles beyond Push there is a landslide of unusually striking character, the road winding about among the mounds and ridges and beneath gigantic trees inclined as if about to fall (Pl. IV, *A*). Numerous cracks cross an adjacent fan and the bluffs above are rent into a tangle of troughs and ridges. Near Courtney Springs (Grace post office) another area of especially marked disturbance is encountered, sharp ridges formed by the slump of the hillside alternating with deep trenches in a most confusing manner. This locality is picturesquely called the "Devils Hens Nest" by the inhabitants. In one of the landslide trenches is a pond, known locally as "Lake in the Hill," about 100 feet long. Originally it must have been much longer, but it has been drained by the erosion of the barrier by its outflowing waters.

Cause.—The cause of the landslides was the disturbance of the somewhat delicate equilibrium existing in the bluff by the earthquake. Geologically the bluff consists of a thick series of shaly clays extending from below the base upward for some distance, these being in turn overlain by less clayey silts, the Lafayette gravels, and finally by the loess. Water soaking downward collected in the more sandy beds above the clays, developing a sort of "lubricating action" at the clay contact. At the same time it produced, by saturating the base of the upper deposits, a zone of easy flowage and slipping. The bluffs, formed by undercutting at an ancient stage of the Mississippi, had not yet been brought by erosion to their normal angle of repose and were in a condition of unstable equilibrium, to destroy which only the shock of the earthquake was needed, and then down came the material in a body. This, it appears, was their mode of origin. It does not mean, however, that no landslides occurred before 1811; there probably were some, for it is known that small ones are still occurring. From the relative ages of the inclined and straight trees, however, it appears that a considerable part of the slipping occurred about a century ago, and it is believed to have taken place mainly at the time of the New Madrid shocks.

WARPING.

UPLIFTS AND DOMING.

The records.—Several of the contemporary accounts of the earthquake note the occurrence of uplifts as well as sinking of the land. Thus Bryan [1] states that "the numerous large ponds which covered a large part of the country were nearly dried up. The beds of some of them were elevated above their former banks several feet, producing an alteration of 10 to 20 feet from the horizontal surface." A. N. Dillard [2] says that "previous to the earthquake keelboats would come up the St. Francis River and pass into the Mississippi [through Little River] 3 miles below New Madrid. The bayou is now dry land." Hildreth [3] describes the heaving of the bottom of the Mississippi as sufficient to turn back the waters. Flint [4] says "a bursting of the earth just below the village of New Madrid arrested the mighty stream in its course," and states further that new islands were created. Still others record the formation of rapids by faults or doming (p. 58). Lyell,[5] who visited the area in 1846, says: "From the mouth of the Ohio to that of the St. Francis, including a tract 300 miles in length, * * * was convulsed to such a degree as to create new islands in the river." In the main, however, he regards the action as one of subsidence, stating that "there are no protuberances of upraised alluvial soil projecting above the level surface of the great plain." In this, however, he was mistaken.

In 1837 Usher [6] described, apparently for the first time, the uplift on the south side of the New Madrid bend (Tiptonville dome), giving a diagram showing the uplift as continuing to the mouth of the Obion River. The best account of this dome, however, is that of McGee,[7] who bases his belief in its existence upon the height of the banks, which are not subject to overflow, and upon the exposure of the underlying clays, which elsewhere along the Mississippi are below water level.

In the course of the writer's studies numerous other elevations above the Mississippi flood plains were examined, including the long, narrow, north-south prairies shown on Plate I. Two other domelike aggregations exist. The larger of these is near Blytheville, in northeastern Mississippi County, Ark., and has a diameter of 7 to 10 miles, while the smaller is on Little River just west of Tyronza Lake and has a diameter of only 2 or 3 miles. No sections showing the lower clays were observed, but the fact that the elevations lie

---

[1] Bryan, Eliza, quoted in Am. Geologist, vol. 30, 1902, p. 78.

[2] J. W. Foster, The Mississippi Valley, Chicago, 1869, pp. 9–22.

[3] Hildreth, S. P., Original contributions to the American Pioneer, Cincinnati, 1844, pp. 34–35.

[4] Flint, Timothy, Recollections of the last ten years, Boston, 1826, p. 224.

[5] Lyell, Charles, Principles of geology, vol. 1, London, 1875, pp. 452–453.

[6] Usher, F. C., Am. Jour. Sci., 1st ser., vol. 31, 1837, p. 296.

[7] McGee. W J, Bull. Geol. Soc. America, vol. 4, 1892, pp. 411–412.

athwart the courses of the streams, in positions which apparently indicate that they can not be the result of differential erosion, gives weight to the doming hypothesis. The three uplifts may be termed, according to the location, the Tiptonville, Blytheville, and Little River domes.

Tiptonville dome.—The Tiptonville dome, so far as can be determined from the sections along the river bank and from the descriptions of Usher [1] and McGee,[2] extends from the vicinity of New Madrid southward to the vicinity of Caruthersville, a distance of 15 miles, and from a point west of the Mississippi to Reelfoot Lake, a distance of 5 to 8 miles. The maximum doming appears to lie in a relatively narrow belt, extending from near the south side of the Mississippi at New Madrid a little east of south to a point 2 or 3 miles south of Reelfoot Lake. The uplift in this belt has been sufficient to raise the surface above the reach of the highest floods. The structure of the dome is shown on the banks of the Mississippi where the river cuts the higher portion. The upper 20 feet or so is composed of the sandy loam, clays, quicksand, etc., which everywhere characterize the alluvial deposits of the Mississippi, below which is exposed a thickness of several feet of stiff bluish-green clays that nearly everywhere underlie the alluvium. These clays are not exposed elsewhere along the Mississippi, although they are encountered in numerous wells.

The configuration of the dome, as pointed out by McGee,[2] indicates that it was—

originally a part of the broad flood plain extending from the mouth of the Ohio to the Gulf, and its exceptional altitude and general conformation suggests a localized uplift. Moreover, several of the dry bayous enter Reelfoot Lake squarely or obliquely, and when this occurs there is no trace of delta building, and both channel and natural levees may be traced for long distances in the lake; indeed, for some distances they may be traced throughout their extent and found to connect in the form of a fairly definite drainage system. This absence of deltas indicates that the uplift or deformation occurred suddenly. Furthermore, it is found that while great cypresses, sycamores, and poplars, sometimes two or three centuries old, grow over the general surface of the dome, no trees older than 70 or 75 years grow within the unoccupied bayous; from which it may be inferred that the uplift occurred at least 70 or 75 years ago, and probably not much earlier.

The amount of uplift, judging from the fact that the land is only 10 to 15 feet above high-water mark, could not have been over 15 or 20 feet. Some of the uplift was almost certainly due to the earthquake of 1811, but if Little Prairie, on which New Madrid is situated, is a part of the dome, the uplift will have to be referred to an earlier date, as New Madrid village previous to the shock was on high land, never covered by the floods.

Blytheville dome.—This dome, which, as previously stated, is 7 to 10 miles in diameter, has the same general characteristics as the

---

[1] Usher, F. C., loc. cit.　　　[2] McGee, W J, loc. cit.

Tiptonville dome, just described, with the exception that its continuity is broken by valleys formed by the meanders of Pemiscot River and by indentations due to former swings of the Mississippi, the position of which is now marked by the bayous known as Clear and Flat lakes. The elevation, if actually a dome as there is good reason to believe, did not result from the shock of 1811, for the Mississippi, which has manifestly had a part in shaping its outline, has not flowed against it since that date. The widening of the Pemiscot Valley by the meandering of the stream is likewise an earlier feature, relatively little change having taken place since 1811. The total uplift is probably not over 10 or 15 feet.

Little River dome.—Little River dome does not differ in general character from the two just described, but has suffered probably less change in outline than the others, the oval shape being still very distinct. Little River meanders indiscriminately through high and low ground in a manner likely to result only from superimposition or from doming of the strata beneath its established bed. The depression through its center seems to be an original one and not the result of erosion. In this locality there is no reason to doubt that the doming was the result, in part at least, of the earthquake of 1811. The uplift was probably not more than 5 or 10 feet.

Other domes.—Besides the more notable domes just described there are several low elevations in the vicinity of the sunk lands which may be of similar character. Near the outlet of Big Lake, in Mississippi County, Ark., just south of the Missouri line, especially, the topography seems to indicate that the subsidence of the lake basin was accompanied by a corresponding elevation immediately to the west, which shut off to a certain extent the original drainage, and gave rise to the present lake.[1]

Cause of uplifts and doming.—The hypothesis that the writer regards with most favor as an explanation of the uplifts and doming, although it must be held as largely lacking in definite proof, assumes a lateral movement of the deposits of the central part of the embayment area toward a fault having the direction and position indicated by Plate I. This movement took place by virtue of a subsidence of the "Mississippi trough," and formed the corrugations represented by the domes and basins shown in figure 18 (p. 108). The matter is further discussed on pages 105 to 109.

DEPRESSION—"SUNK LANDS."

No other feature of the New Madrid region is so conspicuous and striking or so widely known as the so-called "sunk lands," resulting from the local settling or warping of the alluvial deposits of western

---

[1] Morgan, A. E., and Baxter, O. G., Report on the St. Francis Valley drainage project; Bull. Office Exper. Sta. No. 230, U. S. Dept. Agr., pt. 1, p. 11.

A. WATER WEEDS OF SHALLOWER LAKES OF THE SUNK LANDS VARNEY RIVER, MO.

B. RIVER-SWAMP TYPE OF SUNK LANDS FORMED BY NEW MADRID EARTHQUAKE, VARNEY RIVER, MO.

A. YOUNG GROWTH ALONG EDGES OF SUNK LANDS, VARNEY RIVER, MO.

B. CHANNEL OF VARNEY RIVER, MO.

Tennessee, southeastern Missouri, and northeastern Arkansas by the action of the earthquake of 1811. The accounts of eyewitnesses are particularly vivid and tell not only of the major alterations, which can still be recognized after the lapse of a hundred years, but of many minor changes now difficult to distinguish from the normal irregularities of the Mississippi bottoms.

TYPES.

The sunk lands may for convenience be divided into (1) those marked by sand sloughs, (2) those characterized by river swamps, and (3) those covered with lakes of standing water.

The sand sloughs, which are elsewhere described (p. 83), are broad, shallow troughs, generally of considerable length, several feet in depth, and marked by more or less extensive, well-defined ridges covered by extruded sand interspersed with depressions in which the timber has been killed by standing water (Pl. IV, B).

The river swamps include the depressed areas along certain of the streams (fig. 9), the level of which is such that water stands over them for considerable periods, but does not cover them so deep as to prevent the growth of timber. They are therefore characterized by wet-land timber, most of which is young growth, although it may

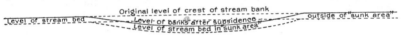

FIGURE 9.—Longitudinal section along stream crossing sunk lands.

include living trees antedating the New Madrid earthquake (Pl. V, A). Often the stumps of characteristic upland varieties of trees killed by the subsidence may be seen. The stream banks in these areas, although submerged for long periods, are often above water during the dry seasons of the year.

The sunk-land lakes are broad, shallow, and essentially permanent bodies of water occurring in depressions of the bottom lands near the Mississippi and other streams or along the depressed channels of streams like the St. Francis. They are simply a stage beyond the river swamps, the water in the lakes being sufficient to cover the banks of the streams, except in seasons of unusual drought, and to prevent the growth of timber in the deeper parts. In the more extensive lakes considerable areas of open water, obstructed only by stumps of the timber killed by the submergence, are frequently found, but in the narrower fluvio-lacustrine types a growth of water weeds often covers the surface. Most of the lakes grade outward into swamps, and there is often a considerable encroachment of young cypress at the sides (Pl. V, A), but the centers of many will probably remain practically free from timber for at least another century. Even where the water weed is most abundant the original channel can usually be traced by a line of open water.

FORM AND TREND.

There is considerable diversity in the form of the sunk-land areas. A few are short and oval, as are Flag Lake, northeast of Kennett (Pl. I), and Flag Prong or Sunk Land Lake (fig. 7), but most of them are long and narrow. Thus Lake St. Francis, although in most places less than half a mile wide, is nearly 40 miles long. The swampy sunk lands west of the lake are of about the same length, though none are more than 2 or 3 miles broad. Buffalo Creek slough, between the lake and the prairie, is at few places more than about one-fourth of a mile wide, but is practically continuous for 35 miles or more. Broader and shorter sunk areas are found at Big Lake and in the East Swamp a few miles east of Campbell, but even in these the linear character is still conspicuous.

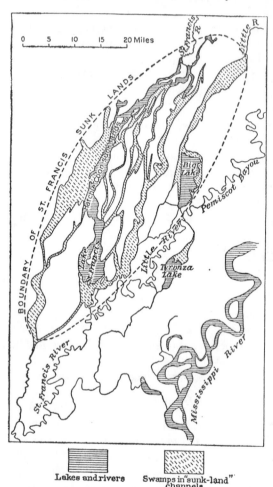

FIGURE 10.—Form of channels in sunk-land district along St. Francis River.

Although generally linear the sunk-land areas are not straight, but are invariably more or less crooked and usually dendritic, many narrow arms branching out and returning, forming a network of channels. This is especially well shown in the St. Francis sunk-land district represented in figure 10 and is in marked contrast to the isolated crescentic forms characterizing the lakes and swamps occupying bayous of the Mississippi, represented in figure 11.

The most irregular of the sunk-land lakes is Reelfoot, which is marked by numerous long points projecting from its shores and by the large bays between them (fig. 12). Its form is probably due to the fact that the basin occupied by the lake is not entirely a structural depression, but includes land over which the waters of the lake were ponded back by an uplift at its southern end.

An examination of Plate I will show that practically without exception the sunk lands have a northeast-southwest trend, the bearing being not far from N. 30° E., agreeing essentially with the trend of

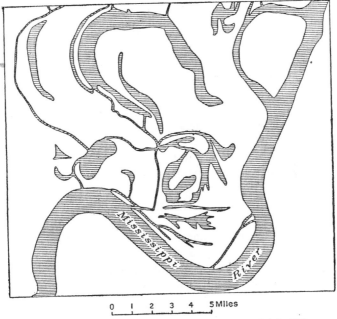

0   1   2   3   4   5 Miles

FIGURE 11.—Forms of bayou-channels and bayou-lakes near Mississippi River.

Chickasaw Bluffs, Mississippi River, the Tiptonville-Blytheville line of doming, the prairie elevations, and Crowley Ridge, thus paralleling both the structural and the topographic features of the region.

AMOUNT OF SUBSIDENCE.

In the sense in which the word subsidence is used in this report it signifies the difference in elevation between the bottoms of the sunk lands and the surrounding alluvial flats, the possibility of elevation of the alluvial flats being for the moment disregarded. The smaller sand sloughs, swamps, and ponds, as in the case of the sand slough leading southwest from Lake St. Francis and the small ponds in secs. 3 and 4 in T. 9 N., R. 5 E. (fig. 7), are often depressed only 2 or 3 feet with reference to the surrounding areas. The lower swamps are not infrequently depressed 5 to 10 feet below the general level of the bottoms, and it is probable that in Lake St. Francis and in other large lakes the depression reaches 15 or 20 feet in places. Certainly the water stands from 6 to 10 feet deep over the original flood plain at many points or from 20 to 30 feet or more over the bottom of the original channel. The deeper parts of Reelfoot Lake, including the channels of the old Reelfoot and Bayou du Chien creeks and the depressions known as basins (fig. 12), are reported to be from 14 to 20 feet deep at low water. It is probable that in this lake the water stands from 2 to 10 feet, or possibly even more locally, over the original land surface.

DISTRIBUTION.

The known sunk lands are practically limited to the flat bottom lands of Mississippi, Little, and St. Francis rivers, and those on each of these streams are found between structural or topographic ridges of greater elevation; the easternmost between the Chickasaw Bluffs and the Tiptonville-Blytheville line of doming, the second between the dome mentioned and the prairie ridge extending from Big Lake to beyond Malden, and the third between the prairie indicated and Crowley Ridge. Sinking doubtless occurred at many other points, as, for instance, at New Madrid, but in general its occurrence can now be recognized only on the bottom lands where the obstruction of drainage makes it apparent.

The general distribution of the sunk-land areas between the structural and topographic ridges has been indicated in the preceding paragraph and it only remains to present a few descriptive notes on the occurrences at various points.

On Plate I are shown a considerable number of sunk-land areas in the St. Francis basin, while a smaller number between Campbell and Cairo are also indicated. The sinking in the latter region was much less than in the region south of Campbell and New Madrid, but the fact that the areas indicated occur within the region of marked disturbance, as evidenced by the numerous sand blows and by the fissures, the latter of which occur at least as far as Charleston (Pl. III); and by agreement in general characteristics with the known sunk lands (fig. 10) rather than with the swamps of the bayou type (fig. 11), leads the writer to class them as sunk lands. In general, however, there is far less water than in the southern sunk lands, and little timber was killed by submergence.

The most northern locality at which conspicuous examples of sunk lands have been reported is in the vicinity of New Madrid. Hildreth[1] states that the site of the town was originally 15 or 20 feet above the floods of the river, but sank so low at the time of the earthquake that the next rise covered it to a depth of 5 feet. According to Bryan[2] the settling amounted to 15 feet, although half a mile below town there was no change in the banks whatever. Bradbury[3] says that

[1] Hildreth, S. P., Original contributions to the American Pioneer, Cincinnati, 1844, p. 35.
[2] Bryan, Eliza, quoted in Am. Geologist, vol. 30, pp. 77-78.
[3] Bradbury, John, Early western travels, Cleveland, 1904, vol. 5, p. 210.

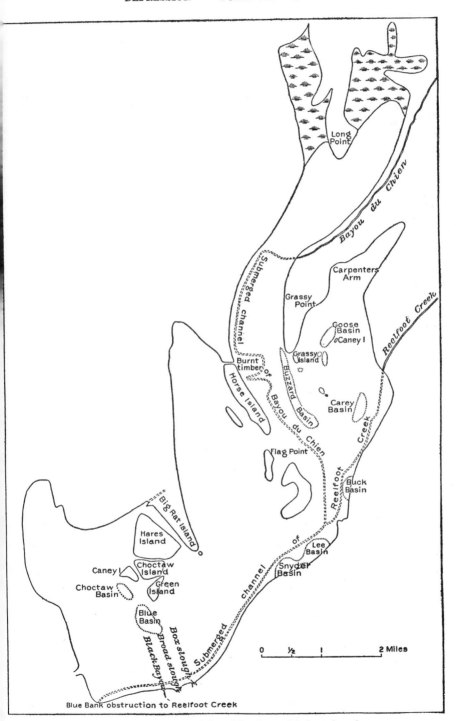

FIGURE 12.—Map of Reelfoot Lake and its submerged drainage channels.

the greater part of the plain on which the town was situated became a lake.

Lyell, who visited the region in 1846, when the evidences were much clearer than at present, says of the district west of New Madrid:

> The largest area affected by the convulsion lies 8 or 10 miles westward of the Mississippi and inland from the town of New Madrid, in Missouri. It is called the "sunk country" and is said to extend along the course of the White Water (Little River?) and its tributaries for a distance of between 70 and 80 miles north and south and 30 miles or more east and west. Throughout this area innumerable submerged trees, some standing leafless, others prostrate, are seen; and so great is the extent of the lake and marsh that an active trade in the skins of muskrats, minks, otters, and other wild animals is now carried on there. In March, 1846, I skirted the borders of the sunk country nearest to New Madrid, passing along the Bayou St. John and Little Prairie, where dead trees of various kinds—some erect in the water, others fallen and strewed in dense masses over the bottom, in the shallows, and near the shore—were conspicuous.[1]

Farther south similar conditions exist. Dillard[2] says:

> I have trapped there [in the region of the St. Francis] for 30 years. There is a great deal of sunken land caused by the earthquake of 1811. There are large trees of walnut, white oak, and mulberry, such as grow on high land, which are now seen submerged 10 and 20 feet beneath the water. In some of the lakes I have seen cypresses so far beneath the surface that with a canoe I have paddled among the branches.

The most northern point at which these sunk lands west of the Mississippi were examined in detail by the writer was near Kennett, Mo., where a trip was made by dug-out on Varny River, a tributary bayou of the St. Francis. Along this river are considerable stretches of water destitute of timber, except for an occasional dead or nearly dead cypress, but covered with a dense growth of water weed, through which a narrow but deep channel meanders (Pl. V, A). Working the boat through the tangle of weeds, it is found that the water about the gaunt dead trunks (Pl. IV, B) is many feet deep. Nothing can be seen of the enlarged butts which normally characterized the cypress trunks from the water surface upward for several feet, but on sounding with an oar the enlargements may be detected.

As the water was, at the time of the writer's visit, at its usual height, it is apparent that there must have been a rise in its normal level of 5 to 8 feet or more since the trees were young. In fact, the original banks of the river appear to be submerged several feet below the water, even in dry seasons, while the average submergence may be as much as 10 or 15 feet. The greater part of the timber in Varny River sunk lands has long since fallen and been covered by the waters, though some dead or nearly dead trees (Pl. V, A) remain. The latter apparently stand in relatively shallow spots where the submergence was not sufficient to kill the cypress immediately, the trees lingering

[1] Lyell, Charles, Principles of geology, vol. 1, London, 1875, p. 253.
[2] Foster, J. W., The Mississippi valley, Chicago, 1869, p. 21.

for years, some even to the present time, before succumbing to their changed environment. Along the edges of the submerged lands the young trees form a dense wall of timber (Pl. VI, *A*), invariably characterized by enlarged butts and contrasting strongly with the straight trunks of submerged trees (Pl. IV, *B*). This young growth has sprung up since the shock and is rapidly encroaching on the swamp (fig. 13). The sharp line of demarcation is shown in Plate VI, *B*, in which the young growth to the right is contrasted to the open portion in which the timber was killed to the left. On nearer approach the details shown by Plate V, *B* and VI, *A* are observed, the enlargements of the butts above the water being especially noticeable in contrast with the straightness of the older trunks at the water's edge.

Apparent evidences of faulting in this region have been cited by Prof. E. M. Shepard, who, describing a trip made several years ago into the swamps, states that "to the east of a north and south line at one point in the swamp the timber grows tall and erect, while to the

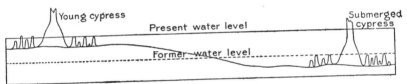

FIGURE 13.—Section showing cypress killed by submergence and young growth springing up in the less deeply submerged areas. The present water level shown is that of normal high water.

west it appears to be submerged to a depth of from 10 to 15 feet."[1] The present writer was unable to verify the occurrence of this supposed fault, and no such features were noted by him in any of the other lakes or sunk-land swamps examined.

Near Caruthersville there was considerable local sinking and a number of small sunk areas occur, but many were filled or rendered unrecognizable by the overflow of the Mississippi before the construction of the levees. Walnut stumps are said to be found just below the surface in swamps along the railroad.

In the "Lake Nicormy swamps," a few miles west of Caruthersville, the conditions are said to be similar to those near Varny River, but the submergence appears to be less and more of the old timber has survived, especially near the edges.

Big Lake, located in Mississippi County, Ark., near the Missouri line and south of Varny River, presents all the usual evidences of forest and other features characteristic of sunk lands submergence. The bottom of the lake is covered with a fallen forest of hardwood of varieties that commonly grow on dry ground, the prostrate trunks of which nearly all lie in the same direction. According to the engineers

[1] Shepard, E. M., The New Madrid earthquake: Jour. Geology, vol. 13, p. 50.

in charge of the St. Francis Valley drainage project, this lake is the most obvious example of sunk lands in eastern Arkansas, although the ponding of the water was probably in part due to an uplift crossing the old drainage lines.[1]

On the Hatchie Coon Sunk Lands, stretching along the St. Francis in Craighead County, Ark., oak, cypress, sweet gum, etc., are found standing in water up to their branches and in some places buried in sand, etc.; it is said that the roots are 50 feet below the surface. All are dead. Elsewhere, especially near Lake City, considerable expanses of water entirely open except for the water weed were noted, the original timber having fallen long ago. Where the water is shallower, however, great trunks, most of them lifeless, still rise to considerable heights, indicating that many of them must have survived long after the submergence due to the earthquake. Plate IV, *B*, shows two of these trunks rising straight from the water with no sign of the enlarged butts, which, however, were detected with an oar a number of feet below the water surface. The encroachment of the young growth is not so conspicuous as on Varny River. The original flood plain lies deep beneath the waters, except in periods of extreme drought, when the waters subside so that they barely show at the surface. At a similar stage of water outside the sunk area the trunks would be normally many feet above the water level.

In Lake St. Francis, a continuation of the enlargement of St. Francis River, just south of the Hatchie Coon Sunk Lands, the conditions are very similar to those just described. The growth, so far as it exists in the lake, is reported to be young, consisting of wet-land varieties which have sprung up since the high-land species were killed by the submergence. Old cypress stumps and submerged trees projecting from the water are said to be found for a distance of one-half to 1 mile from shore.

Submerged trees over which one may float in a canoe are reported in Golden Lake, near Wilson, Mississippi County, Ark., and in other lakes in that vicinity. In Lake Tyronza submerged timber is also common, as it is along Tyronza River for several miles northeast of Tyronza village. Dead Timber Lake, a depressed stream channel connected with Tyronza River, is an open lake with water 6 to 8 feet deep from Tyronza to Deckerville. At times of low water stumps as numerous as the trees in the thickest forest are said to be visible along its bed.

In addition should be mentioned Flag Prong and Sunk Land Lake, secs. 3 and 4, T. 9 N., R. 5 E. (fig. 7). The former is a straight sunk trough about half a mile long, in which stand submerged stumps of mulberry and other highland species. The new growth is mainly

[1] Morgan, A. E., and Baxter, O. G., Rept. on the St. Francis drainage project: Bull. Office Exper. Sta., U. S. Dept. Agr., No. 230, Pl. I, p. 10.

A. STUMPS OF TIMBER KILLED BY SUBMERGENCE CAUSED BY THE NEW MADRID
EARTHQUAKE, REELFOOT LAKE, TENN.

B. ELEVATED CYPRESS NEAR SOUTH END OF REELFOOT LAKE, TENN.

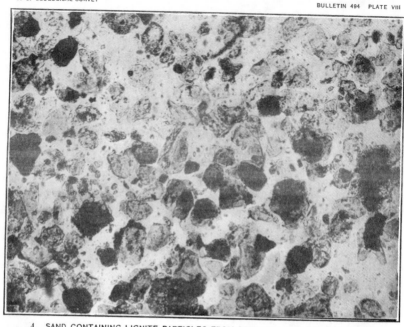

A. SAND CONTAINING LIGNITE PARTICLES FROM DEEP WELL AT MEMPHIS, TENN.

B. SAND CRATERLETS FORMED NEAR SAN FRANCISCO IN THE EARTHQUAKE OF 1906, SHOWING
ORIGINAL APPEARANCE OF SAND BLOWS OF THE TYPE ILLUSTRATED IN PLATE IX.

Photograph by Everett P. Carey.

flags. In Sunk Land Lake the conditions are essentially the same. Log Lake seems to be a depressed bayou as it is much wider than the ordinary channel of the St. Francis and too small to be a Mississippi bayou. No sunk timber is reported in it, but living cypress trees hundreds of years old stand in its bottom. If it is to be regarded as sunk land it must be referred to an earthquake long antedating the New Madrid shocks of 1811. Willow Pond, in sec. 6 of the same township, was marked as sunk land by the land survey of 1845–46, but no stumps are now visible. The bottom is very sandy and supports only flags and willows. The absence of cypress timber, which must have obtained a foothold if the pond was much older than 1811, suggests that notwithstanding the absence of stumps it is to be classed with the sunk lands produced by the New Madrid shock.

The most typical sunk land of the whole earthquake area is Reelfoot Lake in Tennessee. This lake is 8 or 10 miles in length and 2 or 3 in breadth (early statements gave it lengths up to 75 miles and widths of 5 to 10 miles). McGee[1] in a description of the lake says:

Here and there, particularly toward the western side, groves of sickly cypresses spring from its bottom and half shadow the water surface with puny branches and scant foliage, and here and there throughout all portions of the water body, save in the channels of the old bayous, gaunt cypress trunks with decaying branches stand, sometimes a dozen to the acre, numbering many thousands in all. Moreover, between the decaying boles, rising a score to a hundred feet above the water, there are ten times as many stumps, commonly of lesser trees, rising barely to low-water level.

Reference to figure 12, compiled from information collected by the writer, will bring out clearly the shape and general conditions at the lake. On it will be seen the positions of the submerged channels of Bayou du Chien and Reelfoot Creek, at the junction of which an old sycamore stump, many feet in diameter, once standing on high ground, and marking a corner of one of the old Spanish land grants, can still be seen. Here and there are the basins, probably representing, as McGee suggests, old Mississippi bayous or the "lakes" of the inhabitants.

The submergence in Reelfoot Lake ranges from 5 to perhaps 20 feet, although greater depths are reported. The submerged area was well wooded, much of it being covered with species characteristic of dry situations. Most of the timber remained upright after the shock but was gradually killed by the rising waters. The trunks retained their branches for a time, but these gradually dropped away. The better timber was cut off, as shown by the lower stumps in Plate VII, A, but the poorer trees were allowed to stand until they finally broke off, leaving the shattered stumps shown by the view. Throughout practically the whole extent of the lake stumps may be seen projecting above the water, or the remains of old logs may be detected

---

[1] McGee, W J, A fossil earthquake: Bull. Geol. Soc. America, vol. 4, 1892.

beneath the surface. Over large areas the trunks are upright, projecting above the surface by thousands as shown in Plate VII, *A*, from a view taken near Samburg. The visible stumps, however, represent but a small part of the whole, thousands having rotted or broken off below the surface. Many are charred as if burned off. Owen,[1] in fact, says that fires frequently swept from the shores outward through the closely crowded dead timber of the lake. So thick and high was this dead timber as recently as 1855 that Safford[2] stated that even where the lake could not be seen its outline could be traced when looking out over the forest by the lines of dead cypress around its borders. As in the case of the Missouri and Arkansas swamps the difference between the old and young growth is distinct and unmistakable, old straight-sided submerged trunks being frequently seen side by side with a younger growth with the characteristic enlarged butts.

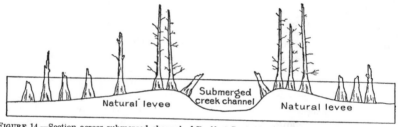

FIGURE 14.—Section across submerged channel of Reelfoot Creek, showing tilted trunks along old banks upright trunks on old bottoms, and living cypresses on slightly submerged natural levees.

Near the submerged channels of Reelfoot and Bayou du Chien creeks the stumps are inclined (fig. 14), their slant being apparently due to the slumping of the banks of the natural levees from which they grew. In other places the timber over large areas was completely prostrated, and where the water is shallow hundreds of trunks may be seen lying below the surface or barely projecting above it. New growth is starting in the shallow parts of the lake, especially along the old natural levees, which are relatively near the surface. Along Reelfoot Creek the land was low and swampy before the earthquake, and cypress constituted the predominating timber. On the higher ground, however, walnut, ash, oak, elm, catalpa, mulberry, etc., abounded, and their stumps may still be recognized among those in the lake.

CAUSE OF SINKING.

The sunk lands may be divided for convenience into local and general areas. The former, commonly known as sloughs, are nearly always associated with extrusion of sand and may have resulted from

[1] Owen, D. D., Rept. Geol. Survey Kentucky, 1854–1855.
[2] Safford, J. M., Geology of Tennessee, 1869.

undermining incident to the ejection of the quicksand beneath the upper alluvial beds or from the contraction of this sand caused by its agitation and readjustment by the earthquake vibrations and the loss of its water. The more extensive sunk lands, however, especially when taken collectively (as the St. Francis group), seem to require a more potent cause, there being far too little extruded matter to account for the depressions. This cause is presumably allied to those producing the doming, which are considered in connection with that phenomenon (pp. 64 and 106). In brief, the sunk lands probably resulted from a warping and lateral movement incident to a subsidence in the floor of the basin, approximately along the line of the faulting that gave rise to the earthquake.

In the formation of Reelfoot Lake, the best known of the sunkland areas, there appear to have been several contributing causes. Several of the earlier writers mention the extrusion of sand along the lower part of Reelfoot Creek in amounts sufficient to clog the channel and obstruct the drainage, and this may have assisted in ponding the waters. The land at the south or lower end of the lake, however, now stands from 10 to 25 feet above the level of the lake bottom, although both appear to have been originally a part of the same approximately level surface. Both sinking and uplift seem to have taken place. The land about Reelfoot Lake has undoubtedly sunk, giving an increased gradient and accelerated velocity to the little streams entering from the east, with the result that the old valleys and fans have been trenched in many places by small but sharp channels. On the other hand, the bottom of Reelfoot Creek channel is a number of feet higher in what was originally the lower part of its course than in the old upper part now covered by the lake. Again, south of Reelfoot Lake cypresses with fully developed knees, such as develop only in water, are found on the high land not now flooded, pointing to a differential elevation of this region. The main movement along the lake appears to have been downward and was due in part to a general depression and in part to faulting. Several of the faults are mentioned on page 58. The uplift at the foot of the lake seems to have formed a part of the general uplift of the Tiptonville dome. The line between the uplifted and submerged lands at the south end of the lake is so sharp that it suggests faulting or at least a very sharp flexure.

West of the Mississippi the conditions were essentially the same, for although, as in the Reelfoot region, the land was low and wet before 1811–12, the waters were much deeper after the earthquake, the ponding being a result of subsidence and the formation of basins combined with a certain amount of drainage obstruction due to local elevation.

EXTRUSION.

RECORDS.

That the phenomena of extrusion, including the ejection of water, sand, mud, and gas, were among the most noticeable features of the earthquake is shown by all published accounts, and this has been fully substantiated by the writer's studies of the extrusion deposits represented by the sand blows and sloughs.

Probably the most reliable account is that of Bringier, the engineer, who says [1] that the water forced its way through the surface deposits—

blowing up the earth with loud explosions. It rushed out in all quarters, bringing with it an enormous quantity of carbonized wood, reduced mostly into dust, which was ejected to the height of from 10 to 15 feet, and fell in a black shower, mixed with the sand, which its rapid motion had forced along; at the same time the roaring and whistling produced by the impetuosity of the air escaping from its confinement seemed to increase the horrible disorder * * *. In the meantime the surface was sinking and a black liquid was rising to the belly of my horse.

Bradbury [2] records a case reported to him by an observer of a chasm which on closing threw water to the height of a tall tree. Similar statements are made by Hildreth,[3] Foster,[4] and Lloyd [5] but are apparently based on current reports rather than on observation.

The quantity of water extruded was enormous. In the vicinity of Little Prairie (Caruthersville), according to Flint,[6] the amount was sufficient to cover a tract many miles in extent from 3 to 4 feet deep. Some districts were still covered at the time of his visit seven years later.

Several writers record the extrusion of gas besides the sand, mud, and water. Hildreth [7] says:

The sulphurated gases that were discharged during the shocks tainted the air with their noxious effluvia and so strongly impregnated the water of the river to the distance of 150 miles below that it could hardly be used for any purpose for a number of days.

CHARACTER OF EJECTED MATERIAL.

As to the nature of the ejected material there are several lines of evidence. On one hand its character is mentioned in nearly all accounts of the disturbance and careful contemporary examinations were made and recorded, while on the other we have at the present time evidences of its nature in the sand blows, sand dikes, and in the material brought up by wells and springs. The material ejected everywhere consisted of sand, with a certain admixture of carbona-

---

[1] Bringier, L., Am. Jour. Sci., 1st ser., vol. 3, 1821, pp. 15–46.
[2] Bradbury, John, Early western travels, Cleveland, 1904, vol. 5, p. 209.
[3] Hildreth, S. P., Original contributions to the American Pioneer, Cincinnati, 1844, pp. 34–35.
[4] Foster, J. W., The Mississippi Valley, Chicago, 1869, pp. 19–25.
[5] Lloyd, J. T., Lloyd's steamboat directory, Cincinnati, 1856, p. 325.
[6] Flint, Timothy, Recollections of the last ten years, Boston, 1826, p. 222.
[7] Hildreth, S. P., op. cit., p. 35.

ceous material, and an occasional foreign fragment, such as the cranium of the extinct musk ox (*Bootherium bombifrons*) later donated to the Lyceum of Natural History of New York.

The sand, which always constituted by far the greater part of the ejected material, consisted, as testified by the sand blows and craterlets, mostly of quartz with a certain admixture of clay and of lignitic and other organic material, which possibly gave rise to the "sulphurous" odors described. Afterward the clay and carbonaceous material was washed out and the sand became bleached nearly white, forming the characteristic white patches and belts that contrast so strongly with the ordinary black soil of the bottoms. The sand seems to have ranged from coarse to fine, a medium grain predominating.

Most of the contemporary accounts speak of the carbonaceous material as "coal," but others speak of it as "carbonized wood" or lignite. The material seen by Lyell near New Madrid is described in one place as bituminous coaly shale (clay), such as outcrops in the river bank and is found in shallow wells 35 feet or so below the surface, and in another as lignite. The best description of its behavior on combustion is given by Mitchill, who examined samples submitted by a correspondent.[1]

I found it very inflammable; it consumed with a bright and vivid blaze. A copious smoke was emitted from it, whose smell was not at all sulphurous, but bituminous in a high degree. Taken out of the fire in its ignited and burning state, it did not immediately become extinct, but continued to burn until it was consumed. While blowed upon, instead of being deadened it became brighter by the blast. The ashes formed during the combustion were of a whitish color and when put into water imparted to it the quality of turning to a green the blue corolla of a phlox whose juice was subjected to its action.

Some specimens of the lignitic matter were coated with a whitish or yellowish substance, suggesting sulphur, but it was probably the sulphate of iron common in lignite and certain coals. Wood not lignitized was also reported by some observers.

The largest pieces of lignite observed by the writer were from ½ inch to 1 inch in length and were obtained from the sand dike at Beachwell near Campbell, described on page 54 and illustrated in figure 8. More commonly the lignite occurs as minute particles mixed with the sand grains, as illustrated by Plate VIII, *A*, which shows the appearance of Tertiary sands from a well at Memphis, as they appear when greatly enlarged under a microscope. The samples were furnished by Prof. E. M. Shepard.

TEMPERATURE OF EJECTED WATER.

Most witnesses say nothing of the temperature of the ejected waters, but positive statements are made by one or two. For instance, both Godfrey Lesieur [1] and a correspondent of Mitchill [2] report lukewarm water extruded from the cracks in the New Madrid area. The extrusion of warm water is also reported by Haywood. [3] This presumably arises from the subterranean warmth at even moderate depths. The mean annual temperature of the region is about 54°, which would be approximately the temperature of the ground-water at the depth of no variation, say 50 feet below the surface. Water of this temperature emerging on a cold December night would be almost sure to feel warm. If it came from any considerable depth the temperature would be about 1° higher for every additional 50 feet of the depth of its source.

ESCAPE OF GAS AND WATER AFTER THE EARTHQUAKE.

In a few places the ejection of water and gas continued for some time after the cessation of the earthquake shocks.

Foster in 1869 [4] notes that "blasts of air and gas yet found their way to the surface through many of the half-filled fissures," and more recently Shepard has maintained that subterranean waters in the form of springs are still being forced up. He says:

A careful study of these streams, especially along the St. Francis, the Little Tyronza, and the Big Bay reveals the fact of the constant escape of water from small openings surrounded by little cones of sand. This is noticeable for miles along the St. Francis and in the Big Bay district, especially on the bluff side of the streams. Deep-seated water, then, is constantly coming to the surface, bringing with it fine sand from below.

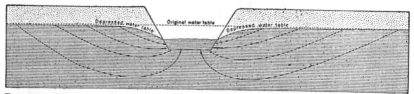

FIGURE 15.—Diagram showing normal movements of ground water, such as give rise to small springs along streams.

The writer visited the region in company with Prof. Shepard, but reached altogether different conclusions. The "small openings surrounded by little cones of sand" are minute springs from 1 to 4 inches in diameter, which, as the writer's hydrologic studies lead him to conclude, differ in no way from the springs that everywhere rise in the bottom of streams under similar conditions. The volume of a single spring is only a fraction of a gallon a minute, and the whole flow of the streams depending upon the springs for their supply was well

[1] Lesieur, Godfrey, quoted in Am. Geologist, vol. 30, 1902, pp. 79–80.
[2] Mitchill, S. L., loc. cit.
[3] Haywood, John, The natural and aboriginal history of Tennessee, Nashville, 1823, introductory chapter.
[4] Foster, J. W., op. cit., p. 25.

under a second-foot. Moreover the numerous wells in the region show that although the water is under artesian pressure it lacks sufficient head to lift it to the surface. The springs can not, therefore, be artesian in nature, and are not of deep-seated origin, but represent rather the water fed from the water table in the ordinary manner as indicated in figure 15.

RESULTING FEATURES.

SAND BLOWS.

Nature.—The term "sand blows" is applied to the low patches of white sand which dot the dark alluvial surface of certain parts of the Mississippi and St. Francis bottom lands in the New Madrid earthquake area, the name being derived from the fact, according to statements handed down from the witnesses of the earthquake, that they were the result of extrusions or blows of sand from fissures produced by the shock. The normal blow is a patch of sand nearly circular in shape, from 8 to 15 feet across and 3 to 6 inches high (Pl. VIII, *B*). Some of the blows are much larger, reaching a diameter of 100 feet or

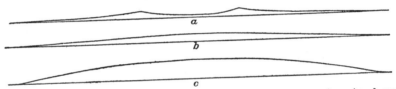

FIGURE 16.—Profiles of sand blows and prairie mounds: *a*, Sand blow with crater depression; *b*, sand blow of rounded type; *c*, prairie mound.

more in the case of the circular types, or lengths of about 200 feet and breadths of 25 to 50 feet in the linear varieties. Many of the larger ones are a foot high, and some may be more. Usually the blows have a low, rounded profile with concave slopes but without trace of a central depression, although crater-like depressions were noted in rare instances. (See fig. 16.) It is assumed that they were all originally connected with fissures, some of which are now closed and afford little evidence of their former existence, although others are still marked by notable dikes or stringers of sand. (Pl. III.)

The material is mainly a medium-white quartz sand, which forms a striking contrast with the dark mucky alluvium on which it rests. With the sand, however, is a greater or less number of particles or chips of lignite, which must originally have given it a somewhat grayish cast. In some instances there seems to have been more or less of a stiff, dark, lignitic clay, practically a shale, brought up with the sand, but this does not appear to be common.

It is desirable to emphasize at this point that the sand blows have no relationship to the prairie mounds, regarding which there has recently been much discussion (fig. 16), although the two have been sometimes confused. The sand blows are confined to the New Madrid area of disturbance, are found only on the lowest of the Mississippi bottoms, are formed of loose white sand without soil, are only a few inches in height, are connected with sand dikes in the underlying alluvium, have concave instead of convex slopes, and some of them have basin or crater-like depressions in their tops. The prairie mounds, on the other hand, are found from Texas to Minnesota, occur on the high terraces and prairies or even on stony hillsides (as at Little Rock), but practically never on the lower floodplains, are composed of loam only slightly sandier or coarser than the underlying soil, are covered by several inches of soil, are often from 1 to 3 or even 4 feet in height, are characterized by convex tops, are unconnected with sand dikes, and have no crater depressions at their crests. One familiar with the two types can distinguish them at a glance.

Situation.—So far as seen the sand blows are limited to the low alluvial lands subject to overflow from the Mississippi or from the St. Francis River. They seldom occur on the higher parts of the bottoms, being generally absent from the Tiptonville, Blytheville, and Tyronza domes or uplifts. They do not occur at all on the prairie ridges, such as those southwest of Charleston, between Sikeston and New Madrid, and east of Lake St. Francis, nor upon the narrow prairie belt along the east side of Crowley Ridge north of Nettleton. Neither are they found on the highlands of Crowley Ridge or Chickasaw Bluffs. Another peculiarity of their distribution is their general absence along the Mississippi, none being noted within 3 or 4 miles of the river bank. This may be due in part to their obliteration by overflowing waters, but this appears hardly probable, and apparently adequate reasons for their absence is afforded by the conditions of their formation (p. 87).

Distribution.—The distribution of the sand blows is indicated on the accompanying earthquake map (Pl. I), that part west of the Mississippi being based mainly on field observations of the writer, and that east of the river on previously published reports. The principal area is oval in shape and extends from a point north of New Madrid on the north to beyond Lake St. Francis on the south. Its shorter diameter reaches from Crowley Ridge on the west to Mississippi River on the east. The area measures 65 miles in length and 25 miles in breadth and has an area of about 1,420 square miles.

The most northern point at which blows were observed was along the railroad between New Madrid and Campbell. They are, however, less conspicuous here than farther south, apparently indicating less, intense disturbance. No distinct blows were observed on the railroad from Sikeston to Dexter a few miles north, although a few indefinite

A. PRESENT APPEARANCE OF SAND BLOW OF CRATERLET TYPE IN THE ARKANSAS
AREA OF DISTURBANCE.

B. COALESCENT OR LINEAR BLOWS OBSTRUCTING DRAINAGE IN THE ARKANSAS
DISTRICT.

A. STUMPS OF TREES KILLED BY DEPOSITS OF SAND.

B. TREES WITH DOUBLE SETS OF ROOTS AT SOUTH END OF REELFOOT LAKE, TENN.

sand patches, possibly representing extrusions, were seen. In the vicinity of Campbell, Mo., 15 miles southwest, however, especially between this town and the settlement of Beechwell, a few miles northeast, they are very numerous and of large size. One covering one-fourth of an acre and from 2 to 3 feet high afforded a site for a house.

South of the village of Lilbourn, a few miles west of New Madrid, to Caruthersville blows are moderately thick. They are first seen rather sparingly near Marston, becoming more numerous at Conran and still more so at Portageville, where the fields are sometimes dotted with them. At Delisle strong blows are seen, continuing, where the conditions are favorable, to Hayti. Between Hayti and Caruthersville they again decrease in number, apparently indicating that their eastern limit is being approached. On the lowlands in the vicinity of Stubtown, just west of Caruthersville, however, a considerable number of blows both of the linear and circular types occur. In several places the blows so obstruct the drainage as to cause the water to collect in shallow pools throughout the wet season. One or two with faint crater-like depressions were observed (Pl. IX, *A*).

On the railroad from Hayti to Kennett fairly strong blows are seen at Pascola and again in weaker development between Lake Nicormy and Kennett. North of Kennett to Campbell the land is somewhat higher than the average, and few blows are seen except beyond Gibson.

Going southward from Caruthersville to Blytheville the railroad runs at no great distance from the eastern limit of the sand-blow area and the extrusions are relatively inconspicuous. On the lowlands near Pemiscot Bayou, west of Blytheville, one linear and several circular blows were seen. Elsewhere the blows were so thick as to touch, giving rise to many irregular depressions, in some of which considerable pools of water accumulate (Pl. IX, *B*). Where the blows were still thicker the whole surface was covered with a continuous sheet of extruded sand. A few weak blows were observed on the outskirts of the Blytheville dome. East of the town there were few blows, their place being taken by the sinks of the type described elsewhere (p. 87).

From Blytheville northwest along the railroad to Paragould blows are constantly in evidence. A short distance west of Chickasawba a fine symmetrical circular blow 100 feet in diameter, 1 foot high, and with a circular depression 15 feet across in the center may be seen. Beyond Pemiscot River sand blows are very numerous and rather weak, but become rapidly larger, higher, and better defined farther west until some fields are reached that are one mass of small, low, sandy mounds. At Hornersville the blows are likewise very numerous, and many lie in a north-south linear arrangement, although not in absolutely straight lines. Elsewhere their distribution is entirely irregular. Many of the blows of this vicinity are marked by barren spots in the corn and cotton fields. Blows are well developed again at Cardwell and Bertig.

North of the railroad from Caruthersville and Paragould sand blows are numerous in the sand-slough region between Grand Prairie and the extension of Lake St. Francis and also, it is said, between the lake and Crowley Ridge as far north as Campbell.

On the railroad running westward from Blytheville to Jonesboro blows are seen at short intervals for the whole distance, especially between Blytheville and Lake City. From Blytheville to Chicka-sawba the blows are relatively scarce, but near Rozelle they begin to be thicker. Between Chicago Mill and Manila a very good crater depression in one of the blows was noted. At Black Oak and Monette the blows are particularly numerous, hundreds of small sand mounds standing out strongly against the dark soil. Some are arranged in long rows as if marking extrusions from a single crack. At Poplar Ridge some blows are seen on relatively high ground. West of St. Francis Lake, between Lake City and Jonesboro, sand is abundant nearly to the edge of the prairie terrace near Nettleton, and low mounds, probably blows, are seen at short intervals.

On the railroad running south from Jonesboro toward Memphis strongly developed blows are seen about Big Bay and Culberhouse, although they are not so conspicuous as in some other localities owing to the fact that here the whole soil is sandy and there is little contrast in color between the blows and the surrounding material. Blows are common also along the St. Francis and Tyronza rivers, where they range from a few feet to one-fourth of an acre in size, and extend, according to reports of surveyors, from the vicinity of Marked Tree northward and northeastward to the railroad extending from Blythe-ville to Jonesboro.

Although the greater part of the evidences of blows still remaining are included in the area described above and outlined on Plate 1, they are by no means confined to this area but are found at many points outside its limits. Bryan[1] describes the extensive extrusion of sand in the New Madrid region. Flint[2] speaks of whole districts in this vicinity which were so covered with sand as to become uninhabitable. Lyell[3] mentions the extruded sand and shale at the edges of fissures. Bringier[4] thus describes the occurrence of blows in the same region:

The whole surface of the country remained covered with holes, which, to compare small things with great, resembled so many craters of volcanoes, surrounded with a ring of carbonized wood and sand. * * * I had occasion a few months after

---

[1] Bryan, Eliza, quoted in Am. Geologist, vol. 30, 1902, p. 77.
[2] Flint, Timothy, Recollections of the last ten years, Boston, 1826, p. 223.
[3] Lyell, Charles, A second visit to the United States, vol. 2, p. 235.
[4] Bringier, L., Am. Jour. Sci., 1st ser., vol. 3, pp. 15-46.

to sound the depth of several of these holes, and found them not to exceed 20 feet, but I must remark the quicksand had washed into them. The country here was formerly perfectly level and covered with prairies of various sizes dispersed through the woods. Now it is covered with slashes (ponds) and sand hills or montecules, which are found principally where the earth was formerly the lowest; probably because in such places the water broke through with more facility.

Blows are not uncommon east of the Mississippi. Haywood says:[1]

The earth in the western parts of west Tennessee opened in several places, and white sand issued from the apertures * * *. Where the white sand was blown up, it lay around the hole in a circular form * * * hillocks of white sand of the size of potato hills. These are all through the Chickasaw country.

In the vicinity of Chickasaw Bluffs, according to Safford,[2] "sand, fine gravel, and fragments of lignite ('coal') were 'blown up' through the fissures and are now found in little ridges or hillocks."

Data collected by the writer leads to the belief that they were found southward nearly to the mouth of the Obion River.

SAND SLOUGHS.

Nature.—Sand sloughs (the word is invariably pronounced "sloos" in the New Madrid region) are linear depressions usually 3 to 5 feet, occasionally more, below the general level of the bottom lands. They are normally characterized by low somewhat ill-defined ridges of sand parallel to one another and to the trend of the depression alternating with shallow troughs, and they collect water into long narrow pools, the largest and deepest of them giving rise to ponds or lakes. The ridges and depressions are as a rule only a few inches in height or depth, but they have had a marked effect on the timber growth. Thus many of the sandy ridges practically refuse to support vegetation and open strips tend to result as the old trees die without their places being taken by younger growth. In the pools much of the old timber, which was largely of highland varieties, was killed. The stumps are still visible in many places, but as yet a new growth has failed to obtain a foothold, although the ponds are often surrounded by willows. The sand sloughs are not infrequently a mile in width, and may be considerably greater. They grade into what may be termed "sand scatters" in which the whole surface of the higher as well as the lower portions of the bottoms is covered with a thin sheet of sand. The material is the same as that of the blows, being a medium white quartz sand, containing a few particles of lignite or chips of a hard shaly clay.

Situation.—The sand sloughs are limited even more strictly than the blows to the lower lands, apparently representing the concentration of the phenomena of which the blows are isolated units. Since depressions are necessary for the production of the phenomena,

[1] Haywood, John, The natural and aboriginal history of Tennessee, Nashville, 1823, introductory chapter.

[2] Safford, J. M., Geology of Tennessee, Nashville, 1869, p. 113.

it follows that the sloughs are always found on the lowest ground and are most conspicuous in the broad, flat bottoms nearest the uplands, rarely near the Mississippi.

Distribution.—The sand sloughs and allied phenomena occur in three main belts, the most extensive being in the St. Francis Valley between Crowley Ridge on the west and the prairie ridge extending from Big Lake on the south to beyond Malden on the north. This area is shown on the general map (Pl. I), and in more detail in figure 10. A second belt almost as extensive, but less strongly developed, lies east of the prairie ridge mentioned and west of the uplift marked by the Tiptonville, Blytheville, and Little River domes. The third belt lies between the Tiptonville dome and the Chickasaw Bluffs, mainly in the Reelfoot Lake region. The first may be called the St. Francis, the second the Little River, and the third the Reelfoot area.

In the St. Francis area the slough extending southwest from Lake St. Francis to the Big Bay at the St. Francis (Pl. I) was examined in 1904. It is a broad sandy belt, some 2 miles in width, occupying a low depression in the bottom lands, marked by numerous long narrow pools, often several to a mile, and characterized by stumps of dead timber. Near Marked Tree several sand sloughs, with the timber either wanting or of small size, are found, but the absence of old stumps suggests that the depression occurred before 1811. The scarcity of young timber is due to the continued presence of the water.

Unfortunately, owing to the high water existing during the more detailed field work in the spring of 1905, the St. Francis sloughs farther north were entirely submerged, and no opportunity for their detailed examination presented itself. From the information that could be collected, however, it appears probable that the sloughs are of much the same character as in the southern part of the area, but with a general increase in the amount of the sand to the north. The sloughs, which are generally associated with the belt of sunk land swamps, are, as shown by the map, much more numerous at the northern end of the area.

In the Little River area, sand sloughs occur in the Big Lake and Lake Nicormy districts, and in the East swamp region east of the West and Rosebriar prairies near Malden. As in the St. Francis area the amount of sand increases toward the north.

In the Reelfoot district, sand probably resulting from extrusion is said to be found at several points beneath the water of the lake, most of them away from the beds of the submerged creeks. Sand ridges several feet in height and surrounded by muddy bottoms are reported by fishermen. At times of flood strong currents from the Mississippi River flow through the lake, however, and are known to have scoured great quantities of sand from the lower end and spread it over the flats to the south, forming the so-called scatters, and it is not impossible that the submerged ridges mentioned are due to the same general cause. There was, however, a considerable extrusion of sand outside of the submerged area, and local sand sloughs doubtless occur.

SAND SCATTERS.

The term "sand scatters" is here applied to the thin surface covering of sand, which can not be differentiated into individual blows or sloughs. The scatters are most commonly developed on low ground, but are also found at higher levels. In composition they are similar to the blows and sloughs, but generally contain less lignite. They are probably of diverse origin, some probably representing confluent blows, others expanded sloughs, and still others the recent wash from the streams. The scatters leading southward from the foot of Reelfoot Lake are of the latter type. In the northern part of the area the so-called scatters are often only sandy phases of the alluvium. This seems to be true in general of the part of the earthquake area north of New Madrid.

The Reelfoot scatters are the most conspicuous and are still in active process of construction or modification. Leading southward from the "Washout" at the extreme southern end of the lake, a broad belt of sand, with occasional pebbles of bronzed gravel resembling the Lafayette, extends southwestward to the Mississippi below Caruthersville, a distance of about 15 miles. Near the lake the sand is in places from 5 to 8 feet in thickness, and has so deeply buried the trees as to destroy them, the dead stumps now projecting from the sand (Pl. X, A). At other points, where the sand bed was only 2 or 3 feet thick, roots have been sent out near the new surface and the trees have survived. In some places a shifting of the currents has removed the sand, showing the trees with two sets of roots, one at the present surface and one at the former level of the sand (Pl. X, B). Over much of the area the sand is destitute of vegetation, barren tracts several acres in extent, marked by large wind ripples and drifting dunes, being not uncommon.

The sand of the scatters has come largely from the "Washout" at the south end of the lake. This is a sharp trench from 15 to 40 feet deep, one-fourth of a mile wide, and a mile or two in length. Great as the trench is, however, it does not seem competent to have furnished all the material of the scatters, and it is suggested that some of the sand may have been scoured from the lake bottom, leaving certain of the supposed ridges of extruded sand.

CAUSE OF EXTRUSION.

The extrusion appears to be of two general types, the first of which may be characterized as violent ejections and the second as quiet extrusion. To the first type belongs the jets described by Bringier,[1] Le Sieur,[2] and other contemporary writers, and to the second the more slow and quiet extrusion giving rise to the sand blows and sloughs.

In regard to the cause, Bringier says:

The violence of the earthquake having disturbed the earthy strata impending over the subterraneous cavities, existing probably in an extensive bed of wood, highly carbonized, occasioned the whole superior mass to settle. This, pressing with all its weight upon the water that filled the lower cavities, occasioned a displacement of this fluid, which forced its passage through, blowing up the earth with loud explosions.

Le Sieur, on the other hand, ascribes the ejection to the bursting of the swells or earth waves which progressed across the surface. Bradbury records extrusions due to the sudden closing of fissures,[3] and several other writers are inclined to similar views.

Of the later writers, Shaler has advanced the theory that "many of the fissures were produced by the escape of gases, which broke forth with all the violence of volcanic eruptions, throwing out great quantities of sand and water." [4]

Extrusion due to the closing of fissures is probably the true explanation of most of the more violent ejections, as it agrees with what would be expected in the case of earth fissures in a thin layer of alluvium resting on a bed of quicksand opening and closing on the passage of large earth waves. It is, moreover, in harmony with the observations of reliable observers in several other more recent shocks. The explosive escape of gases generated by the decay of buried organic matter and disturbed by the earthquake vibrations is a competent and probable supplementary cause of the violent ejections.

The quiet extrusion appears, on the other hand, to be due to the local and temporary development of true artesian conditions, presumably by the unequal settling of the deposits and the production of differential pressures. Although longer-lived than the extrusions described above, they generally last only a few minutes or hours. It is the outflow of waters by quiet extrusion that has carried the sand of the blows and sloughs.

The absence of the blows on the higher lands, such as the prairie ridges, appears to be due in part to the greater thickness of the deposits above the quicksand beds and their greater resistance to fissuring, to their incoherent sandy character which tended to take up the earthquake movements by general readjustments among the grains rather than by fissuring, and to the fact that the head of the

[1] Bringier, L., Am. Jour. Sci., 1st ser., vol. 3, 1821, pp. 15–46.
[2] Le Sieur, Godfrey, printed in Am. Geologist, vol. 30, 1902, pp. 79–80.
[3] Bradbury, John, Early western travels, Cleveland, 1904, vol. 5, p. 209.
[4] Shaler, N. S., Earthquakes of the western United States: Atlantic Monthly, November, 1869, p. 555.

water was generally insufficient to lift it to the higher surface, especially where numerous fissures in the adjacent bottoms afforded lower outlets. The absence of blows in the vicinity of the Mississippi River appears to be due to the fact that the waters and quicksands found an escape by lateral flowage to the stream rather than by extrusion at the surface of the ground.

UNDERMINING.

Fault trenches.—The fault trenches, or canal-like depressions resulting from the settling of a fault block between two adjacent fissures, have been fully described elsewhere (p. 57). As there pointed out, it is probable, especially in the case of the larger trenches at right angles to the streams, that the dropping was permitted by an undermining due to flowage of the underlying quicksands toward the rivers, the channels of which were in many places cut below the quicksand level.

Sand sloughs.—These broad shallow troughs, as has also been pointed out in another place (p. 83), are always marked by extensive accumulations of sand, and their formation, even when due to more general causes, has doubtless been assisted by local undermining due to the extrusion of the sand.

Sinks.—Sinks are among the most conspicuous yet among the rarest of the material phenomena of the New Madrid earthquake, being reported principally in the vicinity of New Madrid. They may be described as circular depressions in the alluvium, originally from a few feet up to 15 yards or more in diameter and from 5 to 30 feet in depth. Lyell, in his account of his second visit to New Madrid,[1] says:

Hearing that some of these cavities still existed near the town, I went to see one of them, three-quarters of a mile to the westward. There I found a nearly circular hollow, 10 yards wide and 5 feet deep, with a smaller one near it, and I observed, scattered about over the surrounding level ground, fragments of black bituminous shale, with much white sand. Within a distance of a few hundred yards were five more of these sand-bursts, or sand blows, as they are sometimes termed here, and, rather more than a mile farther west, near the house of Mr. Savors, my guide pointed out to me what he called "the sink hole where the negro was drowned." It is a striking object, interrupting the regularity of a flat plain, the sides very steep, and 28 feet deep from the top to the water's edge. The water now standing in the bottom is said to have been originally very deep, but has grown shallow by the washing in of sand, and the crumbling of the bank caused by the feet of cattle coming to drink. I was assured that many wagon loads of matter were cast up out of this hollow, and the quantity must have been considerable to account for the void; yet the pieces of lignite and the quantity of sand now heaped on the level plain near its borders would not suffice to fill one-tenth part of the cavity. Perhaps a part of the ejected substance may have been swallowed up again, and the rest may have been so mixed with water as to have spread freely like a fluid over the soil.

[1] Lyell, Charles, A second visit to the United States of North America, London, 1849, vol. 2, pp. 232-233.

Similar sinks are also mentioned by Le Sieur.[1] Still another description is by Bringier,[2] who says:

> The whole surface of the country remained covered with holes, which, to compare small things with great, resembled so many craters of volcanoes, surrounded with a ring of carbonized wood and sand, which rose to the height of about 7 feet. I had occasion a few months after to sound the depth of several of these holes, and found them not to exceed 20 feet; but I must remark the quicksand had washed into them.

The writer in going through other parts of the region saw nothing comparable to the sinks of New Madrid or those described by Bringier, although near Caruthersville the remains of small craterlets were observed in the open fields (Pl. IX, A) and small circular depressions 10 feet or so in diameter and 1 to 2 feet deep were noted at one point in the forest. As it was circular and not irregular in shape and was not associated with any mound it can not be referred to the uprooting of a large tree. The feature to which the term sand blow is now applied is a low patch or ridge of sand, apparently extruded at the time of the earthquake, but not usually associated with any recognizable trace of the opening from which the sand came.

The fact that carbonaceous matter, which must have been extruded from the ground, occurs about the sinks near New Madrid points to their being the orifices "where the principal fountains of mud and water were thrown up" as stated by Bringier, the engineer, to Lyell.[3] As Lyell has pointed out, the sand heaped up about their borders would fill but a small part of the cavity and it is not impossible that the ejected material was so mixed with water as to spread freely like a fluid over the soil. That this was the case with much of the material extruded at the more recent Charleston earthquake was made apparent to the writer from his examination of the earthquake craterlets in 1905.

There is, however, another explanation which the writer would suggest. This is as follows: At the start, the water in the underlying quicksand, which was under temporary pressure due to disturbance of the alluvium by the earth waves, rose through cracks or craterlets and spread sand and carbonaceous materials over the ground. Later, as the pressure was removed, the water subsided and the caving walls filled the cavity produced by the removal of the sand brought to the surface and obliterated the original fissures. Ordinarily the story ended here; but, where the semifluid quicksand outcropped in a near-by river bank, as is the case at New Madrid, there is a possibility of undermining through the flowage of the quicksand toward the stream. The resulting caving tended to be localized where the crust was already broken by fissures, although such localization is not necessary. The fact that the sinks are found only near the river and under conditions similar to those postulated seems to point to the possibility of such an origin. Evidence

---

[1] Le Sieur, Godfrey, op. cit., p. 80.   [2] Bringier, L., loc. cit.   [3] Lyell, Charles, op. cit., p. 231.

supporting this hypothesis is presented by similar sinks under like conditions in the alluvial deposits of Minnesota and other regions which we have no reason to think have been disturbed by earthquakes

HYDROLOGIC PHENOMENA.

Among the hydrologic phenomena associated with the New Madrid earthquakes may be mentioned the extrusion of water from the fissures, the agitation of the water surfaces, the disturbances affecting navigation, and the increase or decrease in the flow of springs. The first of these is properly a phenomenon of extrusion and has been discussed at length under that head. The others, relating more to surface waters, are considered below.

AGITATION OF WATER SURFACES.

Among the phenomena of the earthquake most appalling to the inhabitants of the New Madrid region was the behavior of the river at the time of the shock, and a number of graphic accounts of it have been handed down. As usual, one of the best descriptions is by the English naturalist Bradbury, who states that he was awakened at the time of the first shock—

by so violent an agitation of the boat that it appeared in danger of upsetting. * * * I could distinctly see the river agitated as if by a storm. * * * Immediately the perpendicular surfaces [banks], both above and below us, began to fall into the river in such vast masses as nearly to sink our boat by the swell they occasioned. * * * The river was covered with foam and drift timber, and had risen considerably. * * * Two canoes floated down the river. * * * We considered this as a melancholy proof that some of the boats we passed on the preceding day had perished. Our conjectures were afterwards confirmed.

Capt. Nicholas Roosevelt, already quoted, reported the river unusually swollen and turbid.[1]

Just below New Madrid, according to Lloyd, a flatboat belonging to Richard Stump was swamped and six men drowned.

At times the waters of the Mississippi were seen to rise up like a wall in the middle of the stream and suddenly rolling back would beat against either bank with terrific force. Boats of considerable size were often cast high and dry upon the shores of the river * * *. A man who was on the river in a boat at the time of one of the shocks declares that he saw the mighty Mississippi cut in twain, while the waters poured down a vast chasm into the bowels of the earth. A moment more and the chasm was filled, but the boat which contained this witness was crushed in the tumultuous efforts of the flood to regain its former level.[2]

Hildreth, in relating the experiences of an eyewitness who was on the river 40 miles below New Madrid at the time of the earthquake, says:[3]

In the middle of the night there was a terrible shock and a jarring of the boats * * *. Directly a loud roaring and hissing was heard, like the escape of steam

[1] Latrobe, C. J., The rambler in North America, London, 1836, vol. 1, pp. 107–108.
[2] Lloyd, J. T., Lloyd's steamboat directory, Cincinnati, 1856, p. 325.
[3] Hildreth, S. P., Original contributions to the American Pioneer, Cincinnati, 1844, pp. 34–35.

from a boiler, accompanied by the most violent agitation of the shores and tremendous boiling up of the waters of the Mississippi in huge swells, rolling the waters below back on the descending stream, and tossing the boats about so violently that the men with difficulty could keep upon their feet * * *. The water of the river, which the day before was tolerably clear, being rather low, changed to a reddish hue, and became thick with mud thrown up from its bottom; while the surface lashed violently by the agitation of the earth beneath, was covered with foam, which, gathering into masses the size of a barrel, floated along on the trembling surface * * *. From the temporary check to the current, by the heaving up of the bottom, the sinking of the banks and sand bars into the bed of the stream, the river rose in a few minutes 5 or 6 feet, and, impatient of the restraint, again rushed forward with redoubled impetuosity, hurrying along the boats, now set loose by the horror-stricken boatmen, as in less danger on the water than at the shore where the banks threatened to destroy them by the falling earth or carry them down into the vortices of the sinking masses. Many boats were overwhelmed in this manner, and their crews perished with them. It required the utmost exertions of the men to keep the boat of which my informant was the owner in the middle of the river as far from the shores, sand bars, and islands as they could. At New Madrid several boats were carried by the reflux of the current into a small stream that puts into the river just above the town, and left on the ground by the returning water a considerable distance from the Mississippi. A man who belonged to one of the company boats was left for several hours on the upright trunk of an old snag in the middle of the river, against which his boat was wrecked and sunk. It stood with the roots a few feet above the water, and to these he contrived to attach himself, while every fresh shock threw the agitated waves against him, and kept gradually settling the tree deeper into the mud at the bottom, bringing him nearer and nearer to the deep muddy waters, which, to his terrified imagination, seemed desirous of swallowing him up. While hanging here, calling with piteous shouts for aid, several boats passed by without being able to relieve him, until finally a skiff was well manned, rowed a short distance above him, and dropped downstream close to the snag, from which he tumbled into the boat as she floated by.

Bryan[1] says:

At first the Mississippi seemed to recede from its banks, its waters gathered up like mountains, leaving boats high upon the sands. The waters then moved inward with a front wall 15 to 20 feet perpendicular and tore boats from their moorings and carried them up a creek closely packed for a quarter of a mile. The river fell as rapidly as it had risen and receded within its banks with such violence that it took with it a grove of cottonwood trees. A great many fish were left upon the banks. The river was literally covered with the wrecks of boats.

An informant of Mitchill,[2] who was on the Mississippi River, 87 miles below the Ohio, stated that the stream rose 6 feet from its former level and acquired three times its former velocity. William Shaler, also quoted by Mitchill,[3] says of the experiences of a friend:

He immediately cut his cable and put off into the middle of the river, where he soon found the current changed, and the boat hurried up, for about the space of a minute, with the velocity of the swiftest horse; he was obliged to hold his hand to his head to keep his hat on. On the current's running its natural course, which it did gradually, he continued to proceed down the river, and at about daylight he

---

[1] Bryan, Eliza, quoted in Am. Geologist, vol. 30, 1902, pp. 77–78.
[2] Mitchill, S. L., Trans. Lit. and Philos. Soc. New York, vol. 1, pp. 281–307.
[3] Idem, p. 300.

came to a most terrific fall, which, he thinks, was at least 6 feet perpendicular, extending across the river, and about half a mile wide. The whirls and ripplings of this rapid were such that his vessel was altogether unmanageable, and destruction seemed inevitable; some of the former he thinks, were at least 30 feet deep, and seemed to be formed by the water's being violently sucked into some chasm in the river's bottom. He and his men were constantly employed in pumping and bailing, by which, and the aid of Providence, he says he got safe through. As soon as he was able to look round he observed whole forests on each bank fall prostrate, to use his own comparison, like soldiers grounding their arms at the word of command. On his arrival at New Madrid he found that place a complete wreck, sunk about 12 feet below its level, and entirely deserted; its inhabitants with those of the adjacent country, who had fled there for refuge, were encamped in its neighborhood; he represents their cries as truly distressing. A large barge, loaded with 500 barrels of flour and other articles, was split from end to end and turned upside down at the bank. Of nearly 30 loaded boats only this and one more escaped destruction; the water ran 12 feet perpendicular, and threw many of them a great many rods on shore; several lives were lost among the boatmen.

Flint,[1] in describing the earthquake, says:

A bursting of the earth just below the village of New Madrid, arrested this mighty stream in its course, and caused a reflux of its waves, by which in a little time a great number of boats were swept by the ascending current into the mouth of the bayou, carried out and left upon the dry earth, when the accumulating waters of the river had again cleared their current.

Haywood[2] says that on the first shock the—

waters in the Mississippi near New Madrid rose in a few minutes 12 or 14 feet and then fell like a tide. * * * Spouts of water 3 or 4 inches in diameter sprang from the Mississippi to a great height. In some parts of the Mississippi the river was swallowed up for some minutes by the seeming descent of the water into some great opening of the earth at the bottom of the river. Boats with their crews were engulfed and never more heard of.

Disregarding the element of fantasy in these descriptions, there is little room to doubt that the earthquake produced water waves of considerable size on the Mississippi. They doubtless started from the sides, for the most part, and meeting in the middle produced the sharp wall-like "chop" described at this point. As usual, it was the return wave which did the damage along the shore. That there were upheavals of the bottom is certain, as has been indicated in the discussion of faults and domes, and it is not unlikely that the water was thrown back, giving the appearance of a chasm. There is also no reason to doubt that fissures opened and closed beneath the water as they did on the land, giving rise to large waves by the ejection of water. That waves of great size moved upward against the current is certain, and that the movement of the water was retrograde for the moment, at least in shallow water, is probable. The rise in the river about which there is universal agreement was probably due in part to the waves moving upstream, and in part to a temporary ponding due to local uplifts of the river channel.

---

[1] Flint, Timothy, Recollections of the last ten years, Boston, 1826, p. 224.
[2] Haywood, John, The natural and aboriginal history of Tennessee, Nashville, 1823, pp. 30-33

Not only were the water surfaces agitated by the severe shocks, but in some localities, even to the east of the Mississippi, the preliminary tremors and minor vibrations produced noticeable effects on quiet surfaces. Thus Haywood says, "the ponds of water, where there was no wind, had a troubled surface the whole day preceding any great shock." [1]

The same feature was also observed by Jared Brooks, of Louisville, who, more than anyone else, paid careful attention to the earthquake phenomena. He says [2] he—

stopped on the bank of a deep pond, the surface of which was a perfect mirror to appearance, overhung by lofty trees; it instantly assumed the dull complexion and seemingly the roughness of a file; converging waves were soon raised by the quick motion of the shores, and, contending with each other, caused a curious commotion. The noise produced by the agitation of the trees resembled that of a shower of small hail in the forest.

Further away from the center of disturbance the action was less severe. Describing the trip of Capt. Nicholas Roosevelt, of New York, from Pittsburgh to New Orleans, Latrobe says [3] that while loading the boat from a vein of coal near Yellow Banks, Ind., the voyagers—

were accosted in great alarm by the squatters of the neighborhood, who inquired if they had not heard strange noises on the river and in the woods in the course of the preceding day and perceived the shores shake, insisting that they had repeatedly felt the earth tremble.

It should be stated, however, that nothing is said of any agitation of the waters at this point.

EFFECT ON NAVIGATION.

The conditions of navigation on the Mississippi were much changed by the earthquake. The river was temporarily covered with wreckage and débris, snags and sawyers multiplied, the banks caved, and islands disappeared.

Caving of banks.—Of the caving of the river banks the best account is afforded by Bradbury,[4] who states:

Immediately the perpendicular banks, both above and below us, began to fall into the river. I now saw clearly that our lives had been saved by our boat being moored to a sloping bank. Mr. Bridge, who was standing within the declivity of the bank, narrowly escaped being thrown into the river as the sand continued to give way under his feet; the banks in several places fell within our view.

Capt. Roosevelt, from the deck of the pioneer steamer *New Orleans*, as he was passing down the Ohio along the Indiana shore—

ever and anon heard a rushing sound and violent splash, and saw large portions of the shore tearing away from the land and falling into the river. It was, as my informant said, an awful day; so still that you could have heard a pin drop on the deck.

---

[1] Haywood, John, op. cit., p. 124.

[2] McMurtrie, H., Sketches of Louisville and its environs, Louisville, 1819, Appendix by Jared Brooks, p. 253.

[3] Latrobe, C. J., The rambler in North America, London, 1836, vol. 1, p. 107.

[4] Bradbury, John, Early western travels, Cleveland, 1904, vol. 5, pp. 204–210.

They had usually brought to under the shore, but everywhere they saw the high banks disappearing, overwhelming many a flatboat and raft, from which the owners had landed and made their escape. Here they lay, keeping watch on deck during the long autumnal night, listening to the sound of the waters which roared and gurgled horribly around them, and hearing from time to time the rushing earth slide from the shore, and the commotion as the falling mass of earth and trees was swallowed up by the river.

On reaching the Mississippi they found the channel unrecognizable, everything being changed by the action of the shock. Lloyd,[1] in describing the experiences of another voyager, says that "during the various shocks the banks of the Mississippi caved in by whole acres at a time." Flint[2] says the graveyard at New Madrid was precipitated into the river.

At New Madrid, according to Lyell,[3] the caving of the river was such at the time of the earthquake and in the following years that at the time of his visit the river was flowing over the site of the town. (See fig. 17.)

Disappearance of islands.— Many islands in the Mississippi disappeared at the time of the earthquake. Hildreth says [4] "the sand bars and points of islands gave way, swallowed up in the tumultuous bosom of the river." La-

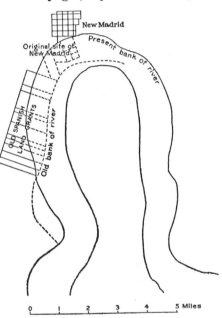

FIGURE 17.—Sketch showing changes in channel of Missis sippi River at New Madrid after the earthquakes of 1811–12.

trobe,[5] describing the trip of the first steamer on the river, says: "The pilot, alarmed and confused, affirmed that he was lost, as he found the channel everywhere altered * * *. A large island in mid-channel, which was selected by the pilot as the better alternative [for anchoring], was sought for in vain, having disappeared entirely." Dow [6] reports the washing away and disappearance of two islands in the New Madrid area. Broadhead [7] quotes from the St. Louis

[1] Lloyd, J. T., Lloyd's steamboat directory, Cincinnati, 1856, p. 325.
[2] Flint, Timothy, Recollections of the last ten years, Boston, 1826, pp. 222-228.
[3] Lyell, Charles, A second visit to the United States, vol. 2, pp. 228-229.
[4] Hildreth, S. P., Original contributions to the American Pioneer, Cincinnati, 1844, pp. 34-35.
[5] Latrobe, C. J., The rambler in North America, London, 1836, p. 108.
[6] Dow, Lorenzo, quoted in Am. Geologist, vol. 30, p. 77.
[7] Broadhead, G. C., Am. Geologist, vol. 30, p. 83.

Globe-Democrat of March, 1902, an article from the papers of Aug. Warner on the disappearance of Island No. 94: "This island was in the lower Mississippi, not far from Vicksburg. * * * In the night the earthquake came, and next morning, when the accompanying haziness disappeared, the island could no longer be seen— it had been utterly destroyed."

The disappearance of the islands, which were usually only a few feet above the water, seems to be due partly to washing and partly to the flowage of the loose, incoherent, water-saturated sands of which they were composed.

Snags and sawyers.—Besides the permanent changes in the banks, islands, and channels, the number of the snags and sawyers was increased or their position shifted. The snags or planters, consisting of partly or wholly grounded wreckage—generally tree trunks—and the sawyers, or those tree trunks grounded at one end while the other rises and falls or sways from side to side in the current, were always dangerous to navigation and were particularly so in the few months following the earthquake. Hildreth [1] states that: "Numerous boats were wrecked on the snags and old trees thrown up from the bottom of the Mississippi, where they had rested for ages. * * * A man who belonged to one of the company boats was left for several hours on an upright trunk of an old snag in the middle of the river." The pilot of the *New Orleans* found, according to Latrobe,[2] the "channel everywhere altered, and where he had hitherto known deep water there lay numberless trees with their roots upward."

Floating wreckage.—Another conspicuous result of the earthquake was the increase in floating wreckage. Bradbury [3] describes the river as full of drift timber after the shock. He found the Devils Channel impassable "from the trees and driftwood that had lodged during the night against the planters fixed in the bottom of the river." One correspondent of Mitchill [4] describes how "the trunks of trees, bedded in the bottom, suddenly rose in great numbers to the surface," during the shock, while Daniel Bedinger wrote to him "of the elevation of innumerable logs and trees from the bottom of the Mississippi." William Shaler, also quoted by Mitchill, mentions "a great multiplication of sawyers." [5]

Combining the partly buried trunks set free by the agitation of the river bottom by the earthquake with the thousands of trees swept into the river by waves or by the caving of the banks, as described on page 96, the floating timber must have been enormous, adding greatly to the difficulties of navigation.

[1] Hildreth, S. P., op. cit., p. 130.
[2] Latrobe, C. J., The rambler in North America, London, 1836, vol. 1, p. 108.
[3] Bradbury, John, Early western travels, Cleveland, 1904, vol. 5, pp. 206–207.
[4] Mitchill, S. L., Trans. Lit. and Philos. Soc. New York, vol. 1, p. 293.
[5] Idem, p. 302.

CHANGES IN SPRINGS.

Among the phenomena of the earthquake were certain changes in the character of particular springs, often at distances remote from the center of disturbance. Col. Samuel Hammond, in a letter to Mitchill,[1] states:

In the county of Christian, Ky., a fine and fresh spring of water was observed to run very muddy for several hours. On examining it, after the feculence had settled, he found it to be strongly impregnated with sulphur, so much so that it was spoiled for domestic uses. Indeed, it had been converted to one of the strongest brimstone springs he ever met with.

P. H. Cole, also writing to Mitchill, says:

In the month of September I visited a spring of about the distance of 14 miles from my residence. It was situated on the bank of a creek that issued forth strong sulphurous water. The smell was evident to a considerable distance. It received its sulphurous impregnation from a very heavy earthquake that occurred in January. Before that event it was a limestone water. On that occasion a new limestone spring broke out about 20 feet above the original spring, and to this day the respective fountains pour forth their calcareous and sulphurous waters in distinct currents. Some springs ceased to run for some time, and others ran muddy several hours after the earth had been convulsed.

In many places in west Tennessee, according to Haywood,[2] old sulphur springs have commenced running again, which some years before were dried up, while several new permanent springs of sulphur water broke out.

ACTION OF THE EARTHQUAKE ON FORESTS.

The modification of the forests of the Mississippi Valley by the New Madrid earthquake was extensive and important, and included the splitting and overturning of trees, their uprooting by landslides and caving banks, their destruction by rushing waters, the uplifting of wet-land species to high and dry positions, and the submergence of highland species.[3]

SPLITTING OF TREES.

The splitting of trees is noted in two of the contemporary descriptions, Bringier describing "trees being blown up, cracked, and split and falling by thousands at a time," and Dillard stating "I have seen oak trees which would be split in the center for 40 feet up the trunk, one part standing on one side of a fissure and the other part on the other, and trees are now standing which have been cleft in this manner."

[1] Mitchill, S. L., op. cit., p. 292.
[2] Haywood, John, The natural and aboriginal history of Tennessee, Nashville, 1823, introductory chapter.
[3] Fuller, M. L., Earthquakes and the forest: Forestry and Irrigation, vol. 12, 1906, pp. 261-267.

DESTRUCTION OF FORESTS BY WAVES AND CAVING BANKS.

The best account of the destruction by waves is that of Bryan, who mentions the falling of trees and describes how an unusual wave of the river in receding "took with it the grove of cottonwoods which hedged its borders. They were broken off with such regularity that in some instances persons who had not witnessed the fact could with difficulty be persuaded that it was not the work of art." Lorenzo Dow adds that thousands of willows were swept off like pipestems about waist-high. Hildreth, in describing the convulsion on the Mississippi, says: "The sand bars and points of islands gave way * * * carrying down with them the cottonwood trees cracking and crashing, tossing their arms to and fro." Bradbury, who was on a boat on the Mississippi, says he could distinctly hear the crash of falling trees, while Devils Channel "appeared absolutely impassable from the quantity of trees and driftwood that had lodged there during the night. * * * The banks in several places fell in, within our view, carrying with them innumerable trees, the crash of which, falling into the river, mixed with the sound attending the shock * * * produced an idea that all nature was in a state of dissolution " A later shock likewise threw great numbers of trees into the river. The effect on the river is also brought out by Latrobe, who, in describing Capt. Roosevelt's trip, says that after the shock the latter found the "channel everywhere altered, and where he had hitherto known deep water there lay numberless trees with their roots upward," while the "trees were seen waving and nodding on the bank, without a wind."

OVERTHROW OF FORESTS BY LANDSLIDES.

Besides the prostration of the forests by the caving of banks along the river, many trees were overthrown by landslides on the steep hillsides, especially along the face of the Chickasaw Bluffs, which border the Mississippi lowlands in western Tennessee. These bluffs are exceptionally steep, largely composed of clay, and when saturated with water, as they often are, present especially favorable conditions for landslides. Their fronts for miles are marked by landslip scars. A study of the age of the trees shows that the greater part of the upright growth on the disturbed surfaces is fairly uniform and a little less than 100 years of age, trees of greater age being in general tilted and partly overthrown. From this it seems clear that the main slides took place about 100 years ago, presumably at the time of the New Madrid shocks. The record of the action of the landslides is still preserved, as indicated, in the older trees as well as in the landslip features. The face of the bluff, which was already nearly as steep as the material could stand, seems to have literally crumbled under the action of the earthquake, great masses slipping downward, carrying with them the immense primeval trees which covered the surface, mingling trees and earth in a confused jumble. Plate IV, *A*, shows trees partly overthrown by the landslides at this time. In this case the original trees survived, gradually straightening until their upper parts again reached an upright position, while the lower parts remained inclined. In other instances, where the original tree was snapped off by the shock, the main trunk has rotted away in the course of years, while a new tree, developed from one of the old limbs or shoots, has taken its place.

GENERAL PROSTRATION OF FORESTS BY VIBRATIONS.

Besides the destruction of the forests by water, landslides, etc., there seems to have been a general prostration in certain localities due to the vibrations alone. For instance, William Shaler, in describing a friend's experiences, says he saw "whole forests on each bank fall prostrate * * * like soldiers grounding their arms at the word of command."

Bringier, in describing his experiences to Lyell,[1] said that in some of the severest shocks, as the waves advanced, he saw the trees bend down and often, the instant afterwards, when in the act of recovering their position, meet the boughs of other trees similarly inclined, so as to become interlocked, being prevented from righting themselves again. In a published account the same observer[2] tells of "the horrible disorder of the trees, which everywhere encountered each other, being blown, cracking and splitting, and falling by thousands at a time."

Very similar conditions in the vicinity of Little Prairie (Caruthersville) are reported by James.[3] "The forest adjoining the settlement at Little Prairie, below New Madrid, presents a singular scene of confusion, the trees standing inclined in every direction and many having their trunks and branches broken."

That such prostration occurs was substantiated by the writer's observations at Reelfoot Lake, over extensive areas of which the trunks are prostrate, although elsewhere standing as upright and stiff as before the shock. As there was no water in the region at the time, and as the land was nearly flat, only the vibrations or accompanying earth waves remain to account for their destruction. In places dozens, if not hundreds, of prostrate trunks can be counted. For comparison, reference should be made to Plate VII, *A*, which shows the upright stumps normally found.

---

[1] Lyell, Charles, A second visit to the United States, vol. 2, p. 231.
[2] Bringier, L., Am. Jour. Sci., 1st ser., vol. 3, 1821, pp. 15–46.
[3] James, Edwin, Account of an expedition from Pittsburgh to the Rocky Mountains, Philadelphia, 1823, vol. 2, p. 326.

DEAD TREES.

A phenomenon of special interest, but somewhat puzzling, is described by Lyell.[1] Skirting the Bayou St. John, he observed—

a great many fallen trees and others dead and lifeless but standing erect. * * * He took me to part of the forest, on the borders of what is called the "sunk country," where all the trees prior to 1811, although standing erect and entire, are dead and leafless. They are chiefly oaks and walnuts, with trunks 3 to 4 feet in diameter, and many of them 200 years old. They are supposed to have been killed by the loosening of the roots during the repeated undulations which passed through the soil for three months in succession.

UPLIFTED TREES.

The uplifted trees, which are occasionally seen in the Reelfoot Lake district, are of special interest because of their rarity, the phenomena of subsidence being much more common. In Plate VII, B, however, is represented an old cypress with a full development of knees, denoting formation in water, the tree being now on high and dry grassy ground, entirely above the reach of the water, except possibly in the time of the highest floods.

SUBMERGED FORESTS.

The phenomena of submerged forests are among the most striking of the earthquake features, and were the subject of some of the most graphic descriptions of the early writers. Even to-day they constitute one of the most conspicuous classes of evidence of the shocks. The best developments are found in the sunk lands of the Varney River in Missouri Big Lake and Lake St. Francis in Arkansas, and in Reelfoot Lake in Tennessee. Many other localities exhibit similar features on a smaller scale. In fact, probable examples may be found in nearly all of the bayous and sloughs connected with the St. Francis River, and their occurrence can not be better seen than by reference to the accompanying map (Pl. I), which shows the swamps and submerged lands as determined by the Mississippi River Commission and verified by the field work for the present report. Reference should be made to the section on "Sunk lands" (p. 64) for detailed descriptions of the phenomena.

AREA OF DESTRUCTION.

Over how great an area the forests were destroyed it is difficult to say at the present time. Reelfoot Lake alone probably originally covered 75 square miles of forest, and the swamps formed at that time west of the Mississippi probably covered 125 square miles more. These two localities alone would comprise more than 125,000

---

[1] Lyell, Charles, A second visit to the United States, vol. 2, pp. 234-236.

acres that were destroyed. The amount of timber lost by the caving of river banks and by the overwhelming of the islands would probably bring the total to 150,000 acres. To this amount still further additions must be made of the areas in which the timber was overthrown by landslides or other related causes. No estimate of the latter can now be made but it was undoubtedly considerable. That the total destruction was sufficient to give earthquakes a place among the enemies of the forest can not be disputed.[1]

EFFECT ON ARTIFICIAL STRUCTURES.

NEW MADRID REGION.

Relatively few details have been preserved in regard to the action of the earthquake upon buildings in the New Madrid region, the natural phenomena evidently making a far greater impression on the minds of the observers than the action on artificial structures. It is known, however, that at the first shock chimneys and other structures of like nature and all loose objects were thrown to the ground, while the damage even to the low cabins was such that it became dangerous to remain in them, and the inmates were obliged to rush out of doors. The larger and more pretentious houses fared quite as badly. Many of the poorly built cabins and houses were destroyed and many fences were thrown down even by the first shock, while certain of the later shocks were even more destructive because of the weakening that all structures had suffered from the preceding shocks.

Flint[2] states that at New Madrid most of the houses were thrown down in an hour, the crumbling being particularly severe during the passage of the large earth waves. As the earthquakes constantly recurred people no longer dared to dwell in houses or to use chimneys, but passed that winter and those succeeding in light bark huts, tents, and other temporary shelters, using camp fires or low ovens to cook their food. The Little Prairie settlement (now Caruthersville) was broken up and the Great Prairie settlement was practically demolished.

According to Stoddard[3] the town of New Madrid was "originally so laid out as to extend, as the French express it, 40 acres in length along the river; the back part was contracted to 20 acres on account of some swamps, and the depth was 16 acres. It contained 10 streets running parallel with the river, and 18 others crossing at right angles. The former were 60 feet and the latter 45 feet in breadth. Six squares were also laid out and reserved for the use of the town, each of which contained 2 acres. * * * A street of 120 feet in

---

[1] Fuller, M. L., Earthquakes and the forest: Forestry and Irrigation, vol. 12, 1906, pp. 261-267.

[2] Flint, Timothy, Recollections of the last ten years, Boston, 1826, p. 222.

[3] Quoted by Beck, L. C., Gazetteer of the States of Illinois and Missouri, Albany, 1823, pp. 299-300.

breadth was likewise reserved on the bank of the river." In 1799 the town had upward of 800 inhabitants, but at one time after the earthquake only two families remained, the remainder having fled. The public works and several streets were carried away by the caving of the river banks and "houses, gardens, and fields were swallowed up." The formation of ponds and the extrusion of sand and water from fissures added to the ruin.

That the destruction was no greater in view of the severity of the shocks was due to the character of the buildings. Speaking of the destruction Flint says:[1]

I infer that the shock of these earthquakes in the immediate vicinity of the center of their force must have equaled in their terrible heavings of the earth anything of the kind that has been recorded. I do not believe that the public have ever yet had any adequate idea of the violence of the concussions. We are accustomed to measure this by the buildings overturned and the mortality that results. Here the country was thinly settled. The houses, fortunately, were frail and of logs, the most difficult to overturn that could be constructed.

DISTANT LOCALITIES.

The destruction by the earthquake, though much less than at the center of the disturbance near New Madrid, extended many hundred miles. Some of the more definite reports of injuries, mainly based on reports of Mitchill,[2] are given below.

St. Louis, Mo.—Several chimneys were overthrown and a number of stone houses split.

Herculaneum, Mo.—Brick and stone chimneys were injured and some broken off and thrown down by the stronger shocks.

Cape Girardeau, Mo.—Several houses were thrown down.[3]

Natchez, Miss.—The plastering in some houses was cracked.

Carthage, Tenn.—Bricks were thrown from chimneys and several were broken and overthrown; the brick courthouse was cracked to the foundation and otherwise injured.

Clarksville, Tenn.—Many chimneys were injured.

Henderson County, Ky.—Nearly every brick or stone chimney in the county was overthrown.

Red Bank (150 miles below Louisville).—Several chimneys were thrown down and others damaged so as to be dangerous.

Louisville.—The damage by the first shock was considerable, gable ends, parapets, and chimneys of many houses were thrown down. Similar destruction was produced by each of the three shocks of "great severity" recorded by Jared Brooks for the week ending December 22, by one in the week ending January 26, one in that ending February 2, and three in that ending February 9.[4]

---

[1] Flint, Timothy, loc. cit.

[2] Mitchill, S. L., Trans. Lit. and Philos. Soc. New York, vol. 1, pp. 281-307.

[3] James, Edwin, Account of an expedition from Pittsburgh to the Rocky Mountains, Philadelphia, 1823, vol. 2, p. 326.

[4] Casseday, Ben, History of Louisville, Louisville, 1852, pp. 121-126.

Cincinnati, Ohio.—The tops of several chimneys were thrown off in town at the time of the first shock, while similar results probably attended the equally violent shocks of January 23 and 27. On February 7 more chimneys were thrown down and wide fissures made in brick walls.[1]

South Carolina.—Cracked and started chimneys were reported at Laurens and Newberry.

Georgia.—Bricks are reported to have been thrown from chimneys.

OTHER PHYSICAL PHENOMENA.

NOISES.

The noises accompanying the more important shocks are among the most noticeable features of the earthquake. Bradbury tells of being "awakened by a tremendous noise" at the time of the first shock and noted that "the sound, which was heard at the time of every shock, always preceded it at least a second and uniformly came from the same point and went off in the opposite direction." Audubon, speaking of one of the more severe shocks, describes the sound as like "the distant rumbling of a violent tornado." Bringier does not mention the subterranean noise, but describes the "roaring and whistling produced by the impetuosity of the air escaping from its confinement" in the alluvial materials. A similar roaring and hissing, like the escape of steam from a boiler, is also described by Hildreth. Eliza Bryan describes the sounds of the shock itself as "an awful noise resembling loud and distant thunder but more hoarse and vibrating." Flint compares the sound of the ordinary shocks to rumbling like distant thunder, but mentions the fact that the vertical shocks were accompanied by "explosions and a terrible mixture of noises." Linn describes the phenomena as beginning with "distant rumbling sounds, succeeded by discharges, as if a thousand pieces of artillery were suddenly exploded," and notes the hissing sounds accompanying the extrusion of the water.

In Tennessee, as described by Haywood,[2] "in the time of the earthquake a murmuring noise, like that of fire disturbed by the blowing of a bellows, issued from the pores of the earth. A distant rumbling was heard almost without intermission and sometimes seemed to be in the air." Explosions like the discharge of a cannon a few miles distant were also recorded, and "when the shocks came on the stones on the surface of the earth were agitated by a tremulous motion like eggs in a frying pan, altogether made a noise similar to that of the wheels of a wagon in a pebbly road."

---

[1] Drake, Daniel, Natural and statistical view or picture of Cincinnati, Cincinnati, 1815, pp. 233-235.

[2] Haywood, John, Natural and aboriginal history of Tennessee, Nashville, 1823, opening chapter.

In the more distant localities we must again rely on the compilation of Mitchill.[1] At Herculaneum, Mo., the noise was described as a roaring or rumbling resembling a blaze of fire acted upon by wind; at St. Louis before the shocks "sounds were heard like wind rushing through the trees but not resembling thunder," while more considerable noises accompanied the shocks. At Louisville the noise was likened to a carriage passing through the street; at Washington, D. C., the sound was very distinguishable, appearing to pass from southwest to northeast; at Richmond similar noises were heard, but they appeared to come from the east; at Charleston there was "a rumbling like distant thunder which increased in violence of sound just before the shock was felt;" while at Savannah the noise was compared to a rattling noise like "that of a carriage passing over a paved road."

From the above it would appear that earth noises were heard at most points where the earthquake was felt. In the region of marked disturbance there were the additional noises made by escaping air, water, crashing trees, and caving river banks. According to the best information the sound in the Mississippi Valley was a some-what dull roar, rather than the rumbling sound of thunder with which it was compared at certain of the more remote localities. In reality, as has been stated to the writer in regard to the recent Jamaica earthquake, although suggesting many of the common noises, it was essentially unlike anything ever heard by the observers before.

ORIGIN AND CAUSE OF THE NEW MADRID EARTHQUAKES.

POPULAR BELIEFS.

Of the various explanations offered by those who speculated on the causes of the shock the volcanic theory was, as usual, by far the most popular. The general nature of volcanic manifestations was more or less understood by everybody, while relatively few had heard of the slower processes of warping and folding and the occurrence of faulting and even those who had seldom appreciated their importance. It is but natural, therefore, that they should turn for an explanation to the known cause which seemed to explain the phenomena best. It is probably to this general belief in the volcanic origin of the shock that the stories of the emission of sparks and similar phenomena are to be attributed.

Even at the time, however, there were some who did not accept the volcanic theory. James,[2] who accompanied Long's expedition to the Rocky Mountains, says:

---

[1] Mitchill, S. L., loc. cit.

[2] James, Edwin, Account of an expedition from Pittsburgh to the Rocky Mountains, Philadelphia, 1823, vol. 2, pp. 325–326.

It has been repeatedly asserted that volcanic appearances exist in the mountainous country between Cape Girardeau and the Hot Springs of the Washita, particularly at the latter place; but our observation has not tended to confirm these accounts, and Hunter and Dunbar, who spent some time at the Hot Springs, confidently deny the existence of any such appearances in that quarter.

Reports have been often circulated, principally on the authority of hunters, of explosions, subterranean fires, blowings and bellowings of the mountains, and many other singular phenomena said to exist on the Little Missouri of the Washita and in other parts of the region of the Hot Springs, but it is easy to see that the combustion of a coal bed or something of equal insignificance may have afforded all the foundation on which these reports ever rested.

Speaking of the New Madrid shock Bringier says: [1]

Several authors have asserted that earthquakes proceed from volcanic causes, but although this may be often true the earthquake alluded to here must have had another cause. Time perhaps will give us some better ideas as to the origin of these extraordinary phenomena. It is probable that they are produced in different instances by different causes and that electricity is one of them; the shocks of the earthquake of Louisiana in 1812 produced emotions and sensations much resembling those of a strong galvanic battery. It will perhaps be pertinent to observe that this earthquake took place after a long succession of very heavy rains, such as had never been seen before in that country.

Nuttall,[2] on the other hand, refers the earthquake to "the decomposition of beds of lignite or wood coal saturated near the level of the river and filled with pyrite."

In the light of our present knowledge of earthquake causes in general and of the nonvolcanic nature of any of the adjacent regions the theory of volcanic origin can be dismissed without further consideration. Electricity can likewise be ruled out as a cause, although certain electrical and magnetic phenomena appear to be associated with most great earthquakes. Aside from the absence of records, geologic or other, of any extensive expulsion of gas we have the testimony of all eyewitnesses to the effect that the expulsion of gases and the associated water was the result and not the cause of the disturbance.

EVIDENCE OF ORIGIN.

One of the best evidences of the origin of the New Madrid earthquake is the nature of the vibrations. If they had resulted from a disturbance within the alluvial deposits themselves, it could have been only from such causes as the expulsion of water and gases, the caving of banks, the slipping of landslides, etc. In regard to the first, it need only be repeated that there is no evidence that any extrusions of water or gas, except those arising in consequence of disruptions brought about by (not causing) the shocks. Of the caving of banks it may be said that had the shores of the Mississippi caved from source

---

[1] Bringier, L., Am. Jour. Sci., 1st ser., vol. 3, 1821, p. 20.
[2] Nuttall, Thomas, quoted by James, loc. cit.

to mouth the vibrations would have been felt only a few hundred feet. Similarly in regard to the landslides. Although the faces of the Chickasaw Bluffs were affected for miles, it was by slipping and not by direct fall, and the jar, if any was produced at all, could have been felt only a short distance. The vertical vibrations accompanying several of the shocks were of a nature differing from any which we can conceive as developing in the unconsolidated deposits themselves.

The best evidence of origin is that afforded by the distance to which the vibrations were felt. It does not seem possible to conceive of a shock originating in soft embayment deposits being transmitted to the hard rocks and thence across the Appalachians to the Atlantic coast on the east and across the central coal basin to Chicago, Detroit, and Canada. The fact that the shocks were strongly felt at these localities seems to point conclusively to a deep-seated origin in rigid rocks. A faulting in the hard Paleozoic rocks seems, therefore, to be the only probable explanation.

LOCATION OF CENTRUM.

Faults, some apparently of relatively recent date, are common in the Ozark Mountains which border the New Madrid area on the northwest and in the southern Illinois and northwestern Kentucky region on the northeast, and the thought naturally suggests itself that some movement in these regions, either a new or the readjustment of an old fault, may have been the cause of the shock. This view was advocated by Prof. Shepard,[1] and was accepted by the writer in an earlier paper.[2] Further study in the field, however, has brought out the fact that the region of marked disturbance is confined to a certain definite area extending from southeastern Missouri to the latitude of Memphis and from St. Francis River on the west to Chickasaw Bluffs on the east, and nowhere reaching within many miles of the edge of the embayment area of soft deposits, as would have been the case if the shock had originated in the hard rocks outside this area. The general trend and shape of the area, taken in connection with the direction of the earth waves, points to a centrum of the original shock along a line having the position indicated on Plate I—that is, a northeast-southwest line extending from a point west of New Madrid to a point a few miles north of Parkin, Ark. The centrum of the heavier subsequent shocks seems also to have been along essentially the same line.

The location of the centrum of some of the later and lighter shocks may have been elsewhere. The motion of one of the shocks at Detroit, for instance, is described as "a pounding up and down instead of oscillating,"[3] which could hardly have been the case if

---

[1] Shepard, E. M., The New Madrid earthquake: Jour. Geology, vol. 13, 1905, p. 61.
[2] Fuller, M. L., Science, new ser., vol. 21, 1905, pp. 349–350.
[3] Mitchill, S. L., Trans. Lit. and Philos. Soc. New York, vol. 1, p. 297.

the shock originated at so great a distance as New Madrid. Similar vertical shocks at Louisville are recorded by Brooks.[1] Drake also notes[2] that during the second year of the earthquake shocks the center of disturbance "seems to have ascended the Mississippi to the Ohio and then advanced up that river about 100 miles to the United States Saline, at which place shocks have been felt almost every day for nearly two years." It is also important in this connection to note that many of the later shocks, while not materially more severe than the first in the New Madrid region, were notably stronger in the more remote regions and were recorded at points in the east, from which no report of the first shock was made.

It seems not improbable, then, that there was more than one center of disturbance northeast of New Madrid in the years following the first shock, probably resulting from disturbance of the local equilibrium by the vibrations originating in the New Madrid area.

ULTIMATE CAUSE.

As shown elsewhere (pp. 109–110), the New Madrid earthquake was but one of a series that is still unfinished, indicating that in all probability it resulted from causes that are still active. Inasmuch as the center of activity of the primary shocks is within the embayment area and well removed from the surrounding areas of consolidated rocks, it seems clear that the ultimate cause lies in forces operating beneath the embayment deposits. The action may be associated either with the processes of folding or warping or incident to a depression and deepening of the basin. In this connection the phenomena of uplift and doming are of the greatest significance and may be reviewed and summarized to advantage.

SIGNIFICANCE OF DOMING.

It is of interest to note that a line drawn through the Tiptonville, Blytheville, and Little River domes agrees in trend with each of the major features of the earthquake region (Pl. I), paralleling the line of the Chickasaw Bluffs and the direction of the Missisippi River on the east and the lines of the prairie ridges, sunk lands, and Crowley Ridge on the west. If the uplift were a few feet higher, a long ridge analogous to the prairie ridges and simulating on a small scale the larger Crowley Ridge would result, suggesting the possibility of a common relationship due either to structure or to erosion.

The Little Prairie Ridge, extending from New Madrid northward for nearly 25 miles, is a direct continuation topographically of the Tiptonville dome, and inasmuch as the river banks near New Madrid

---

[1] Brooks, Jared, in History of Louisville by Ben Casseday, 1852, pp. 121-126.
[2] Drake, Daniel, Natural and statistical view or picture of Cincinnati, Cincinnati, 1815, p. 237.

show a doming of the alluvial deposits parallel to the trend of the prairie, there are good reasons for thinking that the latter may represent the structural as well as the topographic continuation of the dome mentioned. If this is so, it follows that the similar prairie extending from Big Lake to beyond Malden may likewise be of structural origin. On this assumption there would be, beginning on the east, a structural trough occupied by Mississippi River and Reelfoot Lake, a structural ridge marked by the Tiptonville, Blytheville, and Little River domes, a second structural trough occupied by Little River, Big Lake, and Lake Nicormy, a second ridge represented by the Big Lake-Kennett-Malden Prairie, and a third trough occupied by St. Francis River and Lake. Still west of this is the topographic elevation of Crowley Ridge and the basin of Black River. In other words, there is a parallel series of four troughs and three ridges, all of which but one ridge and one trough are believed to be primarily structural in nature. The question arises, may not the two latter be also of structural origin, even if their magnitude is considerably greater? If we disregard the loess of Crowley Ridge a considerable part of the height is taken away, and we have a ridge only about 100 feet high at the most and differing in no way except in size and the extent of its erosion from the lower prairie ridges, and it does not require a great effort to imagine a similar origin for the major ridge. Crowley Ridge has been greatly altered by erosion. Black and other rivers on the west have deepened the associated basins, thus accentuating the elevation of the ridge, and a similar work has been performed by St. Francis, Little, and Mississippi rivers on the east.

The writer does not wish at this time to urge a structural origin for Crowley Ridge, but simply desires to call attention to the occurrence of smaller parallel lines of uplift and depression due to relatively recent warping and to suggest that an earlier and stronger warping of the same nature and in the same direction might have produced a similar uplift along the Crowley Ridge axis, which determined the direction of drainage and the position of the resulting erosion remnant. If this is true, we have the beginning in Mississippi Valley at this point of what may ultimately develop into a synclinorium of great geologic importance.

CAUSE OF UPLIFT AND DOMING.

The uplifts may be conceived as (1) representing the surface indications of disturbances originating in the underlying hard rocks; (2) due to unequal subsidence resulting from undermining; (3) due to horizontal flow of certain of the underlying deposits; and (4) having resulted from lateral movements tending to produce compression.

That the uplift and doming is due to local arching of the bottom of the basin in which the embayment deposits occur is believed to be unlikely, as such movements if communicated through a thousand feet or more of sediments as they needs must be, would be likely to be of more general extent. Moreover, such arching of the hard rocks is a very slow process, while there is reason to believe that the doming took place with considerable suddenness, possibly to a considerable extent during a single period of earthquake disturbance.

Undermining, which may be conceived as resulting from the extrusion of sand from the fissures or by flowage toward the rivers, seems to be even more improbable. It is true, as described elsewhere, that immense amounts of sand were extruded at the time of the shocks; enough, in fact, to cover nearly the entire surface over hundreds of square miles. The layer, however, is usually only 3 to 6 inches deep, and is entirely insufficient to account for the subsidence which in many places amounts to several feet. Locally there was doubtless considerable flowage of the substratum of quicksand toward the streams, but there was no general choking of the rivers from the cause, as would have been the case if amounts sufficient to account for the subsidence had entered them. If there is no adequate basis for the theory of undermining, the latter can not be considered as a cause of differential movement such as might have given rise to domes by the subsidence of the surrounding material.

Horizontal flowage within the substratum of quicksand undoubtedly took place locally, as where there were general movements of the river borders toward the channels, and it is conceivable that movements on a much larger scale may have occurred. Under this hypothesis the domes are to be considered as correlatives of the sunken areas, both being due to movements within the semifluid quicksand. The size of the domes and troughs seems to demand the differential movement of material equivalent to a body of sand 10 feet thick (half of the amount of the difference of surface elevation) for distances amounting to many miles, the distances of the axes of the domes from the adjacent trough axes being from 5 to 10 miles or more. Such a transfer of material is believed to be improbable, although perhaps not impossible. The movement of the quicksand is thought by the writer to have been limited, in most places at least, to half the wave length of the surface undulations accompanying the shocks. In other words, the movements of the quicksand during the shocks are thought to have been similar to the water movements in ordinary waves, the sand particles moving in orbits of similar form without much lateral displacement.

If the doming had been produced by lateral thrust communicated from the hard-rock borders of the basin, we should expect some signs of warping in the broad Tertiary plateau, especially on the east side of the Mississippi, but nothing of the sort is known. If, however, the cause originated immediately under the Mississippi bottoms, the alluvial deposits might be considerably affected without there being any appreciable effect on the uplands. On this point we have the evidence of the earthquake shock, which points to a seat of disturbance along a northeast-southwest line a few miles to the west of the Mississippi. If the fault giving rise to the earthquake was simply the outward expression of a movement of subsidence, as it may well have been, we may conceive of conditions similar to those shown in figure 18, in which D represents a depression formed either through the influence of the faulting or giving rise to it. The result of such a depression would be a settling of the overlying deposits accompanied by a general lowering of the surface about it and a lateral movement in the direction of the arrows toward the center of disturbance, the result of which movement would be the formation of corrugations such as are represented by the domes and allied uplifts. As suggested on page 106, even Crowley Ridge may have originated from similar

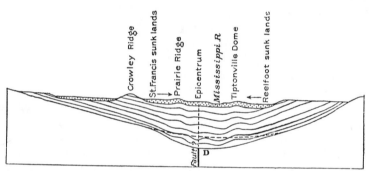

FIGURE 18.—Diagram illustrating possible cause of doming in the New Madrid area.

causes, although its present relief is due largely to erosion. This hypothesis explains the position of the domes and their absence from other areas on the east and west, the anticlinal nature of the disturbance, and accounts for the general preponderance of subsidence over uplift. On the whole it seems to be the most probable of the hypotheses suggested to account for the phenomena of warping and for the earthquakes, which appear to be an incident rather than a general cause of the changes going on.

Although the general movement along the Mississippi is downward, at least differentially, the movement is not continuous. It is probable that as late as the deposition of the Lafayette gravels, in late Pliocene or early Quaternary times, the land stood relatively lower than at present, the deposits named being laid down across the embayment area at an elevation of many feet above the present flood-plain. The distribution of loess affords some reason to think that similar conditions existed nearly down to the time of the Wisconsin glacial stage. If so, there has been removed in relatively recent times a very considerable load from the area, as a result of which the crust would tend to rise until an equilibrium was reached. It is even possible that the shocks of 1811–12 were incidents of an uplift rather than of depression.

CONTEMPORANEOUS DISTURBANCES.

The years 1811, 1812, and 1813 were characterized by unusual seismic activity in many other parts of the Western Hemisphere, as well as at New Madrid. On March 26, 1812, a terrific earthquake occurred at Caracas, throwing down churches and other buildings and destroying 10,000 persons. A little over a week later another heavy shock produced geologic effects of considerable magnitude, over 300 feet of the top of one of the mountains being lost by a landslide. Other shocks were felt at New Grenada and other of the West India islands, while a very important earthquake occurred in California at about the same time. Volcanic action was similarly active. On April 27 the eruption of St. Vincent Soufriere began. During the year preceding more than 200 earthquake shocks presumably of volcanic origin had been felt. Farther away, the island of Sabrina in the Azores was built up to a height of over 300 feet above the sea by a submarine eruption.

A comparison of the dates of the great South American earthquakes with those in Mississippi Valley does not suggest any direct connection. Neither March 26 nor April 5, the dates on which the principal shocks occurred, was characterized by any pronounced disturbance at New Madrid; in fact, both days were unusually quiet. There is a tendency after any great disturbance to produce readjustments to new conditions in surrounding areas, and a series of shocks may be expected to follow in other parts of the same geologic province. There seems, however, to be no possible connection between the New Madrid and Caracas regions, the geologic provinces being entirely unrelated. That the disturbances may each be a surface expression of a single deep-seated cause, such as a general crustal or subcrustal readjustment, nevertheless, is not altogether improbable.

POSSIBILITIES OF FUTURE DISTURBANCES.

In another part of this report a list of the earlier shocks experienced in the New Madrid region is given, and evidences are presented of the existence of earthquake cracks antedating those of 1811 (pp. 11 to 13). In connection therewith should be mentioned the corroborative evidence afforded by Indian tradition, which tells of a great earthquake that had previously devastated the same region.[1]

---

[1] Lyell, Charles, A second visit to the United States, vol. 2, p. 238.

We have also subsequent to the shock of 1811 records of a long line of minor disturbances continuing to the present time, showing that the crust is even now in unstable equilibrium. In other words, the 1811 earthquake was simply one of a series, and further disturbances are still to be expected. Shaler, writing in 1869, said "analogies indicate the probability of its recurrence within a century, since in all those countries which have been visited by great convulsions, where observation has extended over a great length of time, it has been found that their visits may be expected as often as once in a hundred years." [1] Fortunately this prediction has not yet been fulfilled. Any prediction as to when a repetition of the shocks will take place is futile, and it is even possible that no more disturbances will occur for many centuries.

Any severe earthquake originating at or near the center of the 1811 disturbance would be disastrous to such towns as Hickman in Kentucky; Caruthersville, New Madrid, Campbell, and others in Missouri; and Jonesboro, Marked Tree, Osceola, and others in Arkansas, all of which are in or near the area of greatest intensity. The damage would be far greater than from the earlier shocks, owing to the prevalence of brick buildings, and the loss of life would be considerable. The larger cities of Cairo and Memphis would also suffer severely. Memphis, which is within 35 miles of some of the largest fissures in the whole region, namely, those north of Parkin (p. 55), is situated on a loess plain terminating in a bluff about 50 feet high facing the Mississippi River and underlain at water level by a bed of sand saturated with water. These conditions are similar to those which gave rise to the especially heavy destruction at New Madrid, and owing to the greater height of Memphis above the river the danger is accentuated. Cairo, situated on a point between the Ohio and Mississippi, is likewise in an especially dangerous position as regards earthquakes. Such points of land were the very first to give way in the New Madrid shock and to be swallowed by the river, and it is almost certain if a severe shock were to be experienced the danger along the water front would be great. St. Louis would also probably be severely shaken, but it is built on firmer ground and its buildings are less liable to destruction from a shock originating in the New Madrid area because of the remoteness of the point of disturbance. Judging from the action at Herculaneum, however, many structures probably would be seriously damaged, and considerable loss of life might result.

---

[1] Shaler, N. S., Earthquakes of the western United States: Atlantic Monthly, Nov., 1869, p. 559.

BIBLIOGRAPHY OF NEW MADRID EARTHQUAKE.

The following bibliography includes the more important and most trustworthy accounts of the earthquake that have been seen by the writer:

Audubon, John James. Audubon and his journals, New York, 1897, vol. 2, pp. 234-237.

Gives an account of a shock experienced in Kentucky in November, 1812 (probably a mistake in date).

Beck, Lewis Caleb. Gazetteer of the States of Illinois and Missouri, Albany, 1823, pp. 299-300.

Quotes Bringier, Drake, and Nuttall and describes the plat of New Madrid and tells the effect of the earthquake upon the town.

Bradbury, John. Early western travels, 1748-1846; Bradbury's travels in the interior of America, Cleveland, 1904, vol. 5, pp. 204-210.

Gives a detailed account of his experiences on a boat descending the Mississippi and describes the destruction of the forests and the caving of the banks.

Bringier, L. Notices of the geology, mineralogy, topography, production, and aboriginal inhabitants of the regions around the Mississippi and its confluent waters, Am. Jour. Sci., 1st ser. vol. 3, 1821, pp. 15-46.

Gives a description of his experiences in the New Madrid earthquake and of the extrusion of water and other phenomena.

Broadhead, G. C. The New Madrid earthquake: Am. Geologist, vol. 30, 1902, pp. 76-87.

Quotes at length many of the old accounts of the earthquake, but the value of the paper is much impaired by imperfect and incomplete references.

Brooks, Jared. In the "History of Louisville from its earliest settlement till the year 1852," by Ben Casseday, Louisville, 1852, pp. 121-126.

Describes the earthquake phenomena at Louisville and gives a list and classification of the shocks.

————. In "Sketches of Louisville and its environs," by H. McMurtrie, Louisville, 1819, appendix, pp. 233-255.

Gives a complete list of observed shocks, pendulum observations, weather conditions, etc., at Louisville from December 16, 1811, to May, 1812.

Bryan, Eliza. The New Madrid earthquake, abstract by G. C. Broadhead: Am. Geologist, vol. 30, pp. 77-78.

See also Dow, Lorenzo.

Carr, Lucien. American commonwealths; Missouri, a bone of contention, Boston, 1888, pp. 108-112.

Gives an account of the New Madrid earthquake compiled from old narratives, without credit, and describes frauds following the action of Congress in granting new lands to sufferers.

Casseday, Ben. The history of Louisville from its earliest settlement till the year 1852, Louisville, 1852, pp. 121-126.

See Jared Brooks.

Cramer's Navigator, Pittsburgh, 1821, p. 243.

Notes that the river bank for 15 miles above New Madrid sank 8 feet.

Dillard, A. N. In "The Mississippi Valley, its physiography," by J. W. Foster, Chicago, 1869, pp. 19-22.

Relates a number of incidents of the earthquake and describes the phenomena of the submerged lands.

Dow, Lorenzo. "Lorenzo Dow's works" (not seen), Cincinnati, 1850.

Prints a letter from Eliza Bryan giving detailed description of the earthquake and attendant phenomena.

Drake, Daniel. Natural and statistical view or picture of Cincinnati, Cincinnati, 1815, pp. 233-244.

Includes a chronological list of the shocks, a classification by intensities, a general summary of the history of the earthquake, an account of previous disturbances, and a discussion of the contemporary electrical and physical phenomena and the state of the atmosphere at the time of the principal shocks.

Flint, Timothy. Recollections of the last ten years * * * in the valley of the Mississippi, Boston, 1826, pp. 222-228.

Gives a graphic story of the New Madrid shocks and remarks on the conditions existing on his visit seven years later.

———. A condensed geography and history of the western States in the Mississippi Valley, Cincinnati, 1828, 2 vols.

Gives same account as in "Recollections of the last ten years."

———. Extract from travels of Mr. Flint: Am. Jour. Sci., 1st ser., vol. 13, 1829, pp. 366-368.

An abstract of the account in "Recollections of the last ten years."

———. The history and geography of the Mississippi Valley, Cincinnati, 1832, 2d edition, vol. 1.

See "Condensed geography," by Flint.

Foster, J. W. The Mississippi Valley, its physical geography, Chicago, 1869, pp. 19-25.

Quotes the accounts of A. N. Dillard and Timothy Flint at length, appending a few original paragraphs. (See Dillard, A. N., and Flint, Timothy.)

Fuller, Myron L. The New Madrid earthquake, by Edward M. Shepard: Am. Geologist, vol. 35, 1905, pp. 180-181. Review of a paper in Jour. Geology, vol. 13, 1905, pp. 45-62.

———. Causes and periods of earthquakes in the New Madrid area, Missouri and Arkansas: Science, new ser., vol. 21, 1905, pp. 349-350.

———. Comparative intensities of the New Madrid, Charleston, and San Francisco earthquakes: Science, new ser., vol. 23, pp. 917-918.

———. Our greatest earthquakes: Pop. Sci. Monthly, July, 1906, pp. 76-86.

Describes phenomena of New Madrid earthquake and compares them to those of Charleston and San Francisco.

———. Earthquakes and the forest: Forestry and Irrigation, vol. 12, 1906, pp. 261-267.

Describes the destruction of forests by overthrow, submergence, etc., by the New Madrid earthquake of 1811-12.

Goodspeed Publishing Co. History of southeastern Missouri, Chicago, 1888, pp. 53-55; 304-307.

Quotes accounts by Godfrey Lesieur and Eliza Bryan and an unsigned letter in the Louisiana Gazette.

Halstead, Murat. The world on fire, etc., International Publishing Co., 1902.

Quotes previous descriptions of New Madrid earthquake and gives references to places of publication.

Haywood, John. The natural and aboriginal history of Tennessee up to the first settlement therein by the white people, in the year 1768, Nashville, 1823.

Contains an especially graphic account of the New Madrid earthquake in the opening chapter (not included in some other editions of same work). For abstract, see Safford, James M., Geology of Tennessee, pp. 124-125.

Hildreth, Samuel Prescott. American Pioneer, vol. 1, 1842, pp. 139 et seq. (not seen).

———. Original contributions to the American Pioneer, Cincinnati, 1844, pp. 34-35. (Reprint from American Pioneer.)

Gives a detailed account of the experiences of a party descending the Mississippi on a flatboat.

Howe, Henry. Historical collections of the great West, Cincinnati, 1851, vol. 2, pp. 243–246.

Gives Flint's description without specific credit (see Flint, Timothy).

Humboldt, Alexander von. Cosmos, translated by E. C. Otté, London, 1849, vol. 1, p. 207.

Refers to the New Madrid earthquake as one of the few instances of successive shocks throughout long periods in regions remote from volcanoes.

James, Edwin. Account of an expedition from Pittsburgh to the Rocky Mountains under the command of Maj. Stephen H. Long, Philadelphia, 1823, 2 vols., vol. 1, p. 272; vol. 2, pp. 325–326.

Describes the effect of the earthquake on Indians of the upper Missouri country and gives an account of one of the later shocks at Cape Girardeau. The nonvolcanic origin of the shocks is affirmed.

Latrobe, Charles Joseph. The rambler in North America, second edition, London, 1836, vol. 1, pp. 107–108.

Gives an account of the trip of Capt. Nicholas Roosevelt, who was taking the *New Orleans*—the first steamer on the river—down the Ohio and Mississippi at the time of the shock.

Lesieur, Godfrey. (The New Madrid earthquake.) Abstract in "History of southeastern Missouri," Goodspeed Publishing Co., Chicago, 1888.

Abstract in Switzler's "Illustrated history of Missouri from 1541 to 1877," W. F. Switzler, St. Louis, 1879.

Abstract in "The New Madrid earthquake," C. C. Broadhead, Am. Geologist, vol. 30, pp. 79–80.

Linn, Lewis F. (Letter to chairman of committee on Commerce, U. S. Senate) in "Gazetteer of the State of Missouri," Alphonso Wetmore, St. Louis, 1837, pp. 131–142.

Gives a graphic account of the earthquake and its effects.

Lloyd, James T. Lloyd's steamboat directory and disasters on the western waters, Cincinnati, 1856, p. 325.

Gives a general description of the earthquake and some of its associated phenomena.

———. Letter from Cape Girardeau, Louisiana Gazette (Feb. or Mar.?), 1812.

Describes phenomena and destruction resulting at Cape Girardeau from the shocks of Jan. 23 and Feb. 7.

Lyell, Sir Charles. A second visit to the United States of North America, London, 1849, vol. 2, pp. 228–239.

Gives a graphic account of the sinks, fissures, sunk lands, drained lakes, and prostrated forests in the vicinity of New Madrid.

———. Principles of geology, 12th ed., London, 1875, vol. 1, pp. 452–453.

Abstract of the account appearing in the preceding publication.

McGee, W J. A fossil earthquake: Bull. Geol. Soc. America, vol. 4, 1892, pp. 411–413.

Gives a detailed account of the uplift and dome west of Reelfoot Lake, the submerged timber of the region, and the fissures in the face of Chickasaw Bluff.

McMurtrie, H. Sketches of Louisville and its environs, Louisville, 1819, pp. 233–255.

Gives an appendix containing complete records of earthquakes by Jared Brooks. See Brooks, Jared.

Mitchill, Samuel Latham. A detailed narrative of the earthquakes which occurred on the 16th day of December, 1811: Trans. Lit. and Philos. Soc. New York, vol. 1, pp. 281–307.

A compilation of reports of the earthquake from all parts of the United States, especially from the eastern cities.

Musick, John R. Stories of Missouri, American Book Co., New York, 1897, pp. 143–150.

Contains a detailed account of the New Madrid earthquake compiled from early descriptions, but without specific credit being given.

Nuttall, Thomas. A journal of travels into Arkansas, Philadelphia, 1821, pp. 46–47, 58.

Gives an account of a visit to the earthquake region in 1818 and notes the frequency of shocks at that time. Describes the destruction at New Madrid, Little Prairie (Caruthersville), and Big Prairie.

Owen, David Dale. Report of the geological survey in Kentucky, made during the years 1854 and 1855, Frankfort, 1856, pp. 117–119.

Gives descriptions of earthquake features in the vicinity of Reelfoot Lake.

—— First report of a geological reconnaissance of the northern counties of Arkansas, made during the years 1857 and 1858, pp. 31, 203.

Notes the occurrence of numerous earth cracks, sand blows, and associated lignite in Poinsett County, and of earth cracks in Greene County, due in part to the shrinking of the underlying argillaceous strata and in part to the slumping effects of former earthquake action.

Perkins, J. H. Annals of the West, Cincinnati, 1846, pp. 520–524.

Quotes in full the account of Hildreth (see Hildreth, S. P.) and mentions that the first steamboat on the Mississippi (see Latrobe, C. J.) was nearly overwhelmed.

Safford, James M. Geology of Tennessee, Nashville, 1869.

Gives an account of earthquake features especially landslides in western Tennessee and reprints an account of the earthquake and its phenomena.

Shaler, Nathaniel Southgate. Earthquakes of the western United States: Atlantic Monthly, November, 1869, pp. 549–559.

Quotes Bradbury's description and gives Drake's list of shocks at Cincinnati. States that centrum moved during continuance of shocks from west of the Mississippi to the mouth of the Wabash River. Mentions fissures 100 feet deep in Obion County, Tenn.

—— Kentucky, Boston, 1885, p. 44.

Contains a brief and somewhat inaccurate description of the New Madrid earthquake.

—— Notes on the bald cypress: Memoirs Mus. Comp. Zool., vol. 16, No. 1, 1887, pp. 1–15.

Notes death of cypress when water covers knees and quotes Reelfoot Lake, Tenn., as an example, the submergence being due to the New Madrid earthquake. Many trees are living whose knees are nearly but not quite submerged.

Shaler, William. (Letter to S. L. Mitchill): Trans. Lit. and Philos. Soc. New York, vol. 1, pp. 300–302.

Gives an account of the experiences of a friend on board a boat on the Mississippi.

Shepard, E. M. The New Madrid earthquake: Jour. Geology, vol. 13, 1905, pp. 45–62.

Quotes several of the early accounts, describes the earthquake features as now existing, and discusses their relation to artesian conditions, concluding that the sinking was due to undermining by circulating earth waters.

Smith, Edward Darrell. On the changes which have taken place in the wells situated in Columbia, S. C., since the earthquakes of 1811–12: Am. Jour. Sci., 1st ser., vol. 1, 1818, pp. 93–95.

Failure began after dry seasons and the year after shock, the loss being only partly restored in the following wet seasons. Author does not assume earthquake to be the cause.

Switzler, W. F. Switzler's illustrated history of Missouri from 1541 to 1877 (not seen), St. Louis, 1879.
Reprints a graphic account of the earthquake and earthquake phenomena by Godfrey Lesieur.

Usher, F. C. On the elevation of the banks of the Mississippi in 1811: Am. Jour. Sci., 1st ser., vol. 31, 1837, pp. 294–296.

Warner, Aug. (Disappearance of Island No. 94), St. Louis Globe-Democrat in March, 1902, quoted by Broadhead, G. C., Am. Geologist, vol. 30, p. 83.
Describes the disintegration of the island during the shock.

Wetmore, Alphonso. Gazetteer of the State of Missouri, St. Louis, 1837, pp. 131–142.
Prints a long letter by Lewis F. Linn, United States Senator, giving a graphic account of the earthquake and its results and gives a few original remarks stating that earthquakes were still felt every two weeks or so.

INDEX.

COVER STORY
ESCAPE FROM LITTLE PRAIRIE, DECEMBER 1811

In the early morning hours of December 16, 1811, when the first of the great New Madrid Shocks struck, the small village of Little Prairie was especially hard hit. The town of Caruthersville, founded after the earthquakes in 1857, is near there today, but the original settlement of Little Prairie is not to be found on any modern map. It disappeared during that series of upheavals, never to be seen again. Records disagree as to whether it was upon the first, second or tenth severe temblors of that day, but after one of them the town began to sink until it was covered by two to four feet of water.

Approximately 100 people had to wade eight miles to the nearest dry land in a cold December, leaving their houses in a shambles, collapsed in the turbulent waters. Carrying children on their shoulders, packing what small provisions they could, they stumbled through those muddied waters, never knowing when the next step would plunge them into a submerged crevasse or cause them to stumble over a tree stump. Snakes, wolves, possums, and raccoons, creatures of all kinds were likewise swimming to safety. The small band walked through devastated swamp forest for eight days, arriving at New Madrid some twenty three miles to the north, on Christmas eve, only to find the town there also in ruins, the residents all camping out of doors. Luckily, no one was drowned or killed in Little Prairie, but the town was lost forever.

The drawing for the cover of this book is by Mark Farmer, a Cape Girardeau artist, who has tried to capture the desperation of that scene as the families of Little Prairie fled for their lives from what had been their quiet sylvan settlement on the banks of the Mississippi. A historical account of this exodus can be read in this book, The New Madrid Earthquakes by James Penick, available from the Center for Earthquake Studies, $10.95 ppd.

Little Prairie wasn't the only town to be totally destroyed by those earthquakes. Another was Big Prairie, Arkansas, near present-day Helena, which also disappeared in a similar fashion. Even the original site of New Madrid has also vanished beneath the waters of the Mississippi. The great shock (M_S-8.8) of February 7, 1812, caused the town to subside 15-20 feet after which it was swept away without a trace in the Spring floods of that year.

Dr. David Stewart